Mantua

Mantua

Electa

How to use this guide.

Introduction
The first part of this guide consists of an introduction which gives a brief summary of the historical events linked to the building and development of the city of Mantua.

The Visit
The second part of the guide is made up of a series of itineraries, six of them within the city and one devoted to the localities in its environs. This section begins with a *general plan*. In the key are indicated places, churches, and palaces that are described in the guide. The numbers and letters permit their rapid identification on the general plan.

The *places* and *monuments* described are printed in bold type.

The *works of art* mentioned are printed in italics.

The *artists* cited are printed in relation to the historic monument in which they worked, by their dates their birth and death or the period of their activity that is known to us.

Each itinerary commences with a *plan* of the urban area through which the route passes, and is described by an introductory text that draws attention to its most important sites and monuments.

Sites and *monuments*, easily identifiable on the plan by means of their geographical coordinates, are then listed in logical sequence, in relation to the territory through which the route extends. The history, artistic events, alterations, and current state of each one are described.

Texts
Giorgio Bombi

Translation
Huw Evans

Filmsetting of the text and reproduction of the illustrations by Bassoli Olivieri Prestampa, Milan

Contents

History and Development of the City

The origins of Mantua appear to belong to the realms of legend: the story goes that it was the daughter of the prophet Tiresias, Manto, fleeing from Thebes after the death of her father, who arrived in this land "in the middle of the marsh" and founded the city. The legend, taken up even by Dante (*Inferno*, XX, 56-93), was more widely believed than others which attributed the foundation of the city, sometime between the 6th and 5th centuries B.C., to Manto's son Ocnus, or to an infernal Etruscan deity named Mantu.

There are scanty traces of prehistoric settlements in the area. However, excavations carried out in the vicinity of Forcello, about 15 km from Mantua, have brought to light the remains of an ancient Etruscan market city. It seems certain that this place, on the Mincio, was one of the furthest points reached by the inhabitants of Etruria in their expansion to the northeast, in the 6th century B.C. Etruscan domination, which was responsible for the flowering of craft and trading activities over the course of the 5th century B.C., came to an end in 388 B.C., following the invasion of the Cenomani Gauls. This was followed in turn by Roman conquest in 220 B.C.

In 41 B.C., part of the territory was confiscated, divided into centuries, and allotted to colonists. It appears that the *cardo*, one of the two principal axes on which the division of the land into regular lots was based, lay along the western side of what is now Piazza Sordello, but this is a hypothesis which has yet to be confirmed. At the time the settlement was an *oppidum parvum*, a small fortified town, which occupied roughly the area of the present Piazza Sordello and its immediate surroundings. Its inhabitants depended primarily on farming for their existence. After the fall of the Roman empire, the territory was invaded, in the 4th and 5th centuries A.D., by Germanic peoples: there is a tradition that it was in the region of Mantua, and more precisely in the vicinity of Governolo, that Pope Leo I the Great halted the advance of Attila and his Huns. Marcomanni, Visigoths, Huns, and Ostrogoths occupied the territory in successive waves, but without leaving traces on the urban layout of Mantua.

The first recognizable elements in the urban structure date back to the early Middle Ages and correspond to the original nucleus, located on a low ridge bounded by the waters of the Mincio. The defensive walls of this town were demolished in 602 by Agilulf, King of the Langobards, and brought to light a few years ago in the course of works of restructuring.

After Charlemagne's victory over the Langobards, the territory passed to the Franks. In the middle of the 9th century, it became part of the Attonian mark, that is to say subject to the jurisdiction of the Attoni margraves of Canossa, by the will of Emperor Louis II. Mantua too was caught up in the investiture contest, which was settled in the end by local forces: as happened in other fiefs belonging to the Attoni, the vassal milites were granted certain privileges and a degree of autonomy. These were to be the seeds of the communal freedoms. The Commune of Mantua, established in 1116 by Emperor Henry V, took part in the struggles between the Emperors Frederick I Barbarossa and Frederick II and the communes,

taking the side of the latter after a period of uncertainty.
It was during the period of the communes that Mantua developed into a center of political and commercial importance.
The course of the Mincio was regulated, by means of a major operation of hydraulic engineering under the supervision of Alberto Pitentino (1190), to form four lakes (Lago Superiore, Lago di Mezzo, Lago Inferiore, and Lago Paiolo), while the Rio canal defined the new limit of the city that had now spread beyond the first circle of walls. Surrounded by water on three sides and reinforced by imposing defensive works, the city was considered impregnable for centuries. The political center remained the zone around the present-day Piazza Sordello, where the richest families, the Bonacolsi and Gonzaga, had built their palaces, but the city now stretched as far as the suburbs in the south thanks to the formation of a trading zone along the road to Cremona. Over the course of the 13th century, Mantua succeeded in maintaining its autonomy, in spite of serious threats from the Communes of Ferrara, Modena, Reggio, and Verona, and to carry on with its own process of evolution, notwithstanding the struggles that took place among the aristocratic families for control of the city.
In 1272, the Bonacolsi united to gain ascendancy over the city, which they retained through a policy of internal reconciliation and external alliances up until 1328, when the Gonzaga drove their adversaries out of the city in a single night, occupying all the buildings situated between the Cathedral and what is now Via Accademia, the stronghold of the Bonacolsian *signoria*.
The last of the Bonacolsi, Rinaldo known as "Passerino," was killed and his sons incarcerated for the rest of their lives in a tower of Castellare, the modern Castel d'Ario. From that day, 16 August 1328, until 1707, the history of Mantua was bound up with the Gonzaga dynasty, rich landowners who had at first sought power as a means of strengthening their economic situation, but then came to conduct themselves as out and out princes. Having consolidated their hold over the city, in 1433 the Gonzaga, with Gianfrancesco, obtained the title of

Domenico Morone, The
Expulsion of the Bonacolsi;
the event, which took place
during the night of 16 August
1328, marked the beginning
of the Gonzaga dynasty's
dominance.

marchese from Emperor Sigismund, with the right of hered-
itary transmission of rule. With Ludovico II, Lord of Mantua
from 1444 to 1478, they turned the city into one of the liveliest
centers of the Renaissance: Donatello, Leon Battista Alberti,
Luciano Laurana, Luca Fancelli, and Andrea Mantegna were
all summoned to the court. The basilicas of Sant'Andrea and
San Sebastiano were built to designs by Alberti, the Palazzo
del Broletto was renovated, and the Palazzo Ducale extend-
ed, preparing the way for the works of the Domus Nova. The
city, which had already overflowed the urban limit of the Rio,
formed a new perimeter bounded by the five gates known as
Porta San Giorgio, Porta Mulina, Porta Pradella, Porta Pusterla, and Porta Cerese. It was subdivided into twenty historic quarters, traces of which are still to be found today: Aquila
(Eagle), Grifone (Griffon), Cammello (Camel), Orso (Bear),
Monticelli Bianchi (White Hills), Monte Nero (Black Mountain), Serpe (Snake), Leopardo (Leopard), Mastino (Mastiff),
Corno (Horn), Falcone (Falcon), Leone Vermiglio (Vermilion
Lion), Cigno (Swan), Bove (Ox), Unicorno (Unicorn), Pusterla (Postern), Cavallo (Horse), Cervo (Deer), Rovere (Oak),
and Nave (Ship). An already splendid Mantua was enriched
by new works of art by Ludovico II's successor, Federico I,
and to an even greater extent by Francesco II, who became
marchese in 1484. He was assisted in his work of patronage by
the cultured and refined Isabella d'Este, whom he married in
1490, when she was only fifteen. Under Francesco II's son and
successor, Federico II, who was made a duke by Emperor
Charles V in 1530, Mantua encountered the artist who was to
bequeath the richest legacy to the city, Giulio Pippi, better
known as Giulio Romano. Active in the city from 1524 until his
death, in 1546, Giulio Romano, one of the undisputed masters
of Mannerism, worked on the Corte Nuova of the Palazzo Du-

*The Camera degli Sposi in
the Palazzo Ducale: detail
of the frescoes by Andrea
Mantegna showing the court
of Ludovico II Gonzaga.*

Piazza Sordello. In the background the Duomo. The crenelated building on the left is Palazzo Castiglioni, traditionally known as Palazzo Bonacolsi.

Domenico Brusasorchi, Saint Margaret (ca. 1550), in the Duomo of Mantua.

cale, on the Duomo, on country houses and residences of the aristocracy, on secular buildings like the Pescherie, on the planning of the city, and on Palazzo Te, his masterpiece.

The splendor of the Gonzaga court continued under the dukes Francesco III, Guglielmo, and above all Vincenzo I (1587-1612), who filled Mantua with yet more works of art: such as the Basilica Palatina, the Ala dei Mori in the Palazzo Ducale, the Galleria degli Specchi, and the Salone degli Arcieri.

The crisis brought about by the folly and prodigality of the last dukes, already acute enough in 1627 to oblige Vincenzo II to sell part of his collection of paintings to King Charles I of England, reached its height when the same Vincenzo II died in 1627 without direct heirs. This left open the problem of succession in Mantua as well as in a territory of such strategic importance as Monferrato. Europe was in the midst of the Thirty Years' War and dynastic disputes were frequently resolved by armed force rather than on the basis of legal right. In Mantua the succession should have gone to Carlo Gonzaga, Duke of Nevers and member of a cadet branch of the family that had moved to France, but this candidature, which threatened to favor French interests, was regarded with suspicion by Emperor Ferdinand II of Habsburg. So an army of landsknechts was despatched to drive the legitimate Duke Carlo out of Mantua. After a long siege, they took the stronghold on 18 July 1630 ("sack of Mantua"). But the heavy damage inflicted during this bloody pillage was of little significance compared with the tragic legacy left behind by the imperial troops: the same plague as ravaged Milan and Lombardy.

In an ironic twist of history, Carlo di Gonzaga-Nevers was later to become the Lord of Mantua in any case, bequeathing the duchy to his son Carlo II. It then passed into the hands of Ferdinando Carlo until 1707, when the last duke was accused of "Treachery" to the emperor for having failed to fulfill his obligations of vassalage, and was deposed. From that moment on, Mantua was assigned to Austria, while Monferrato was taken

over by the Savoys. Under Austrian administration the city underwent a new period of growth, evidence for which is provided by such significant realizations as the dome of Sant' Andrea, designed by Filippo Juvara; the work carried out in the churches of San Barnaba and San Maurizio; the Palazzo Cavriani and Palazzo dei Gesuiti, designed by Alfonso Torregiani; Antonio Bibiena's Teatro Scientifico with the adjoining Accademia Virgiliana, to a design by Giuseppe Piermarini; and the apartments of the Arazzi and the Imperatrice in the Palazzo Ducale.

Conquered after a long siege by Napoleon's troops Mantua returned to Austria in 1814. Along with Peschiera, Verona, and Legnago, it became the main axis of the system of fortresses known as the "quadrilateral." The outstanding monuments of these years, which were characterized by the draining of the Paiolo basin, while the Diga dei Mulini and the Ponte di San Giorgio continued—and still continue—to mark the limits of the Lago Superiore, Lago di Mezzo, and Lago Inferiore, are Luigi Canonica's Teatro Sociale and some fine buildings designed by Giovan Battista Vergani.

The last part of the 19th century, which for Mantua signified union with the kingdom of Italy after the third war of independence, in October 1866, was marked by an expansion into the hinterland, along the routes leading to the nearby cities of Cremona, Modena, Parma, Brescia, and Padua. The destruction of the walls built by the Gonzaga, probably an unnecessary measure, has eliminated a precious point of reference in the urban fabric. However Mantua, owing to its peculiar structure, has the advantage of having been forced to preserve its historic center and of having a direction of expansion that was at once unavoidable and self-limiting. Perhaps the greatest problem is that of harmonizing the magnificent traces of the past, with the requirements of an urban center that has to meet precise needs of an administrative character and that does not want to be turned into a museum.

1   2   3

A

B

Lago Superiore

C

Via Alberto Pitentino

P.za S Fra d'Ass

60

STAZIONE Piazza
FF.SS.   Don E.Leoni

59   58

L.go di
Porta Pradella

Corso Vittorio Emanuele

Via Giovanni Pascoli

Via Silvio Pellico

Viale 7 Dicembre

Piazzale
A. Mondadori

Via Cremona

Viale Monsignor Luigi Martini

Via Cremona

Via Cremona

L.go
Petrarca

Viale Manzoni

Viale Fiume

Piazza
G. Bazzani

51   52

Via Napoleone Mambrini

Via Ciro Menotti

Viale Vittorio Alfieri

Viale L. Da Vinci

Viale Piave

Via Luca Fancelli

Via Della Conciliazione

D

Via Teresa Valenti

Dosso del Corso

Viale Pompilio

Viale Fiume

Viale Istria

Viale Asiago

Via Istria

Via Hermada

Viale Carso

Viale Plave

Viale Pasubio

Via Enrico Dugoni

Via Della Conciliazione

Via Fratelli Griol

Dosso del Corso

Via Cantoni

Strada Chiesanuova

Viale Belgioioso

P.tta
T. Zaniboni

P.za
A. De Gasperi

Viale Fiume

Viale Sabbioni

Viale
Podgora

Viale Asiago

Piazzale
Antonio Gramsci

Viale D.Chiesa

V. Rimembranze

XXIV

Viale Della Repubblica

Viale Gorizia

Viale Gorizia

Viale Oslavia

Viale A. Parilla

Viale G. E. Gobio

Viale Luigi Vaschi

P.za
D'Acquisto

V. Brigata Mantovati

Viale Generale

Viale Montello

P.le
V. Veneto

57

Viale Monte Grappa

Piscina
Comunale

E

Strada Chiesanuova

Viale Belgioioso

Viale Indipendenza

Viale Pompilio

Viale Pietro Albertoni

ISTITUTI
OSPEDALIERI

Viale Oslavia

Viale Fiume

Via Giorgio

S.usan

Viale Montenero

Teliera

Viale Gino Vesci

Viale

Strada Trincerone

Via Gian Battista V

Via Sabioneta

Via Tamassia

Via F. Finetti

Via Val D'Ossola

Viale Pompilio

Canale Paiolo

Via Federico Amadei

Strada Chiesanuova

Via C. delle Stiviere

F

Strada Trincerone

Via Marcello Donati

Strada di Circonvallazione Sud

0   200   400
                 m

Margil

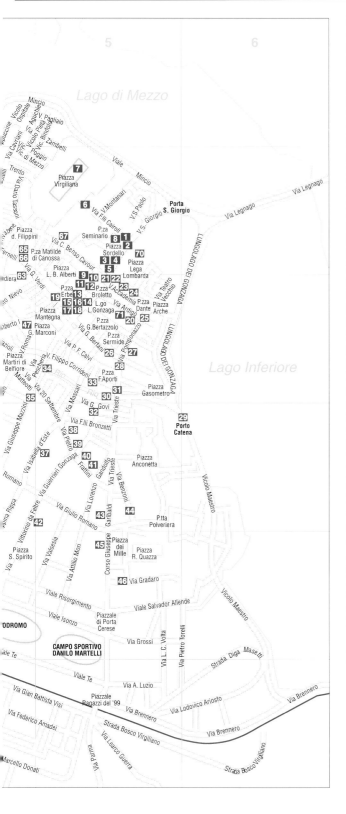

1. Torre della Gabbia; 2. Palazzo Acerbi; 3. Palazzo Castiglioni; 4. Palazzo degli Uberti; 5. Palazzo Vescovile; 6. Palazzo del Seminario; 7. Museo Francesco Gonzaga; 8. Duomo; 9. Palazzo del Podestà; 10. Museo Tazio Nuvolari; 11. Palazzo del Massaro; 12. Arengario; 13. Università dei mercanti; 14. Palazzo della Ragione; 15. Torre dell'Orologio; 16. Rotonda di San Lorenzo; 17. Merchant's House; 18. Torre del Salaro; 19. Basilica of Sant'Andrea; 20. Biblioteca Comunale; 21. Accademia Virgiliana; 22. Palazzo dell'Accademia; 23. Teatro Scientifico; 24. Biblioteca accademica; 25. Palazzo della Finanza; 26. Palazzo del Rabbino; 27. Palazzo Sordi; 28. San Martino; 29. Porto Catena; 30. Rio; 31. G.B. Bertani's House; 32. Norsa Synagogue; 33. Santa Maria della Carità; 34. Pescherie; 35. Santa Teresa; 36. Monastero del Carmelino; 37. San Lorenzino; 38. Menozzi House; 39. Palazzo Valenti Gonzaga; 40. Andreasi House; 41. Sant'Egidio; 42. Santo Spirito; 43. Santa Paola; 44. Sant'Apollonia; 45. Santa Caterina; 46. Santa Maria del Gradaro; 47. Lanzini House; 48. Teatro Sociale; 49. Palazzo Aldegatti; 50. San Maurizio; 51. San Barnaba; 52. Giulio Romano's House; 53. Palazzo di Giustizia; 54. Palazzo del Governo; 55. Mantegna's House; 56. San Sebastiano; 57. Palazzo Te; 58. Sant'Orsola; 59. Ognissanti; 60. San Francesco; 61. Palazzo d'Arco; 62. Palazzo Ippoliti di Gazoldo; 63. Palazzo Arrivabene; 64. Palazzo Arrigoni; 65. Palazzo Canossa; 66. Madonna del Terremoto; 67. Palazzo Barbetta; 68. Palazzo Cavriani; 69. San Gervasio e Protasio; 70. Palazzo Ducale; 71. Palazzo degli Studi.

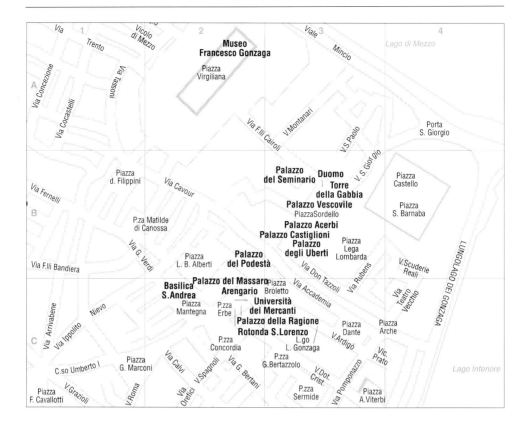

Through the Squares of the Historic Center

Piazza Sordello, Piazza Broletto, Piazza Erbe, Piazza Mantegna, and, a little further to the north, Piazza Virgiliana, with only a few tens of meters separating one from the other, are the vital centers of Mantua, the focal points around which stand some of the best-known historical and artistic buildings of the city.

Piazza Sordello, heart of the urban structure, is surrounded by some of the oldest and most interesting of Mantua's monuments: you can begin your visit by admiring the so-called "Bonacolsian palaces," that is to say the buildings of the Bonacolsi era, though renovated in later periods, that mark the western edge of the square. Starting from the corner furthest away from the Cathedral, you can see the **Torre della Gabbia** and beneath it the **Palazzo Acerbi**, then **Palazzo Castiglioni**, probably the residence of the Bonacolsi family, the 15th-century **Palazzo degli Uberti** with the charming Vicolo Bonacolsi, and the 18th-century **Palazzo Bianchi** and **Palazzo Vescovile**. Crossing Via Fratelli Cairoli, you come to the facade of the **Seminario** (Seminary) and the **Duomo** (Cathedral), which closes Piazza Sordello to the north and whose interior deserves a visit as well.

Coming out of the cathedral, you continue along the eastern side of the square for a visit to the various buildings of the **Palazzo Ducale** (to which the second itinerary is devoted): the **Magna Domus** and the **Palazzo del Capitano**, which give onto the square, and, set further back, the **Castello di San Giorgio**, which houses the celebrated **Camera degli Sposi**.

On the opposite side to the cathedral, after passing under the arch of the Voltone di San Pietro, you can see the porticoes of Piazza Broletto: on the right, Via Cavour, with the aforementioned Torre della Gabbia, adjacent to Palazzo Guerrieri (early 16th century) with its facade patterned by pilaster strips and traces of pictorial decorations, and then, at no. 79, **Palazzo Andreasi** with its brickwork cornice and marble portal dating from the 15th century. Lastly, at no. 35, there is the 17th-century palace formerly belonging to the **Conti Mantelli**; on the left, Via Accademia, the southern limit of Mantua in the 11th and 12th centuries.

Continuing under the porticoes, you come to **Piazza Broletto**, onto which face the **Palazzo del Podestà** with the **Torre Comunale**, the **Palazzo del Massaro**, the arch of the **Arengario**, and the old seat of the **Università dei Mercanti**. From here you can pass into **Piazza Erbe**, the traditional site of the fruit and vegetable market, flanked by palaces with porticoes. Outstanding among these are the **Palazzo della Ragione**, with the adjoining **Torre dell'Orologio**, the **Rotonda di San Lorenzo**, and the **Torre del Salaro**. The whole is dominated by the side of the imposing basilica of **Sant'Andrea** whose facade forms the edge of **Piazza Andrea Mantegna**: this church is the largest in Mantua and its interior, filled with extraordinary works of art, is well worth a visit.

Piazza Sordello. In the background the Duomo, on the right the crenelated Palazzo del Capitano and the Magna Domus, which form part of the Palazzo Ducale.

On the following page: The corner of Piazza Sordello with the Voltone di San Pietro, the palaces of the Bonacolsi, the so-called "Tower of the Cage" and the dome of Sant'Andrea.

PIAZZA SORDELLO (B-3). Dedicated to the Mantuan troubador and poet, who was actually a native of Goito (ca. 1200-ca. 1269), mentioned by Dante in Canto VI of the *Purgatorio*, the square occupies the site of ancient Mantua. On the south side, opposite the **Duomo**, can be seen the so-called **Voltone di San Pietro**, the arch of one of the gates in the original city walls. Created in the 14th century by demolition of the houses that formerly crowded the area, the square is rectangular in shape. The northern side is closed by the facade of the **Duomo**. On the opposite side stands the arch leading to Piazza Broletto and Piazza Erbe, as well as to Via Cavour and Via Accademia. Looking toward the cathedral with your back to the arch, you can see that Piazza Sordello is bounded on the left by a row of old palaces. The first, on the corner of Via Fratelli Cairoli, is the **Palazzo Vescovile** (Bishop's Palace); in front of it, on the other side of Via Cairoli, is visible the neoclassical facade of the **Seminario**, constructed in 1825 to a design by Giovan Battista Vergani (1778/1788-after 1841). Adjacent to the Bishop's Palace stands the **Palazzo degli Uberti**, followed by the narrow Vicolo Bonacolsi. This is traversed by an arch that links the Casatorre, a building from the end of the 13th century, to the nearby **Palazzo Castiglioni**, also known as Palazzo Bonacolsi. Finally there is the facade of **Palazzo Acerbi**, dominated by the **Torre della Gabbia** (Tower of the Cage). The eastern side of Piazza Sordello, on the right-hand side if you are facing the cathedral, is bounded by the buildings of the **Palazzo Ducale**, and in particular, by the oldest structures in the complex, the Magna Domus and the crenelated Palazzo del Capitano.

TORRE DELLA GABBIA (B-3, Piazza Sordello). Tower ("of the Cage") built during the signoria of the Bonacolsi, at the beginning of the 14th century. A large iron cage was inserted about halfway up the tower, which is 55 m high, in the second half of the 16th century. This was used to expose malefactors,

Palazzo Acerbi, on the left, and Palazzo Castiglioni, which form the sides of Piazza Sordello.

for a certain period, to the gaze of the city's inhabitants: the chronicles tell of a pickpocket who was imprisoned in it for over three months in 1576.

PALAZZO ACERBI (B-3, Piazza Sordello). One of the residences of the Bonacolsi family, Lords of Mantua from 1272 to 1328, it still displays traces of the 13th-century brickwork windows on the facade overlooking the square. Inside the palace, the family chapel was decorated, in the early 14th century, with a cycle of frescoes painted by an artist of the Giotto school, but these were removed and dismembered during the last century. From the building rises a quadrangular tower, known as the "Tower of the Cage" ever since the Gonzaga, toward the end of the Cinquecento, built an iron cage into it that was used as a "pillory" for wrongdoers.

PALAZZO CASTIGLIONI (B-3, Piazza Sordello 10-12). Erected according to tradition by the Bonacolsi, Lords of Mantua from 1272 until 16 August 1328, it was more probably acquired by Pinamonte Bonacolsi in 1281. During the 19th century, the building passed to the Conti Castiglioni, noble descendants of Baldassare Castiglione (1478-1529), a native of Casatico in the Mantuan region, the author of the *Cortegiano*.

The brickwork facade, surmounted by battlements, has elegant, round three-mullioned windows and two portals: the first, at no. 10, has a pointed arch; the second, at no. 12, dating from the Renaissance, had been taken from the destroyed monastery of San Giovanni and bears the symbols of Isabella d'Este (1474-1539), wife of Francesco II Gonzaga and mother of Federico: the alpha and the omega united and a triangular candelabra with a single candle.

Palazzo Vescovile, formerly Palazzo Bianchi. Note the Atlantes supporting the marble balcony.

PALAZZO DEGLI UBERTI (B-3, Piazza Sordello). Built in a late Gothic style on the corner of Piazza Sordello and Vicolo Bonacolsi by the Uberti family, which came to Mantua after the Ghibellines were driven out of Florence, the building retains traces of the original 14th-century structures, incorporated into a succession of reconstructions. These are especially apparent in a number of windows and cornices on the side facade, overlooking the alley.

PALAZZO VESCOVILE (B-3, Piazza Sordello). Also known as Palazzo Bianchi, after the Marchesi Bianchi who had it built between 1776 and 1786, it has been the bishop's see since 1823. The facade has two powerful Atlantes at the sides of the entrance, supporting a marble balcony. Inside there is an impos-

The neoclassical facade of the episcopal seminary, overlooking Via Cairoli.

Piazza Virgiliana, with the monument to Virgil designed by Luca Beltrami and realized in bronze by Emilio Quadrelli.

ing grand staircase and a large number of frescoed rooms, some of them by the Mantuan artist Giuseppe Bazzani (1690-1769).

PALAZZO DEL SEMINARIO (B-3, Via Cairoli). Situated just a few meters from the Duomo, the Seminary building has a fine neoclassical facade erected in 1825 by Giovan Battista Vergani (1778-after 1841). Continuing along Via Cairoli, you enter **Piazza Virgiliana**.

PIAZZA VIRGILIANA (A-2). Laid out from 1735 onward on a site created by the draining of a marsh connected with the Lago di Mezzo and redesigned by Paolo Pozzo (1741-1803) in 1797, it was named after Virgil in 1801 at the behest of the French commandant General Millis, who had a column bearing a bust of the poet erected in the square. This monument was destroyed by the Austrians, who in 1820 constructed an elegant amphitheater in the part closest to the lake. This was demolished in turn in 1927 to make room for a new *monument to Virgil*, designed by Luca Beltrami (1854-1933) and executed in bronze by Emilio Quadrelli (1863-1925), while the marble groups at the sides, portraying his *Heroic Poetry* and *Pastoral Poetry*, are by Giuseppe Menozzi. A number of old buildings face onto the square and the adjacent Via Virgilio, such as the palace at no. 55, designed in 1795 by Paolo Pozzo, today the seat of the **Museo Francesco Gonzaga** and formerly known as the monastery of Sant'Agnese, as well as the ones at no. 25, the Ospedale Grande until 1797, which contains three 15th-century cloisters, and at no. 17, designed by Giovan Battista Vergani (1778/after 1841).

MUSEO FRANCESCO GONZAGA (A-2, Piazza Virgiliana). Formerly the convent of Sant'Agnese, it was restructured by Paolo Pozzo (1741-1803), who left some parts like the *inner cloister* intact but added on a *neoclassical facade*. It is named after Francesco di Gonzaga di Bozzolo who was bishop of Mantua from 1599 to 1620. It houses many precious exhibits: sacred objects from the churches of Mantua, such as a *Madonna and Child* in silver (13th century), a French coffer dating from 1533, 14th- and 15th-century silver crosses, a group of Italian suits of armor of the 15th and 16th centuries from the sanctuary of the Madonna delle Grazie, ciboria, monstrances, devotional prints, votive offerings, gold work belonging to the Gonzaga, a Flemish tapestry, an 18th-century statue of Saint Anselm, and *sinopie* (preparatory drawings for frescoes) of the *Deposition* by Correggio and the *Ascension* by Mantegna, both from the church of Sant'Andrea.

DUOMO (B-3, Piazza Sordello). Dedicated to Saint Peter, the cathedral was built on top of earlier sacred buildings, including a Romanesque church known to have stood on the site in the 11th century.

The latter's 14th-century facade, attributed to the brothers Jacobello and Pier Paolo Dalle Masegne (documented from 1383 to 1409) was reproduced in a famous painting by Domenico Morone (ca. 1442-after 1517) depicting *The Expulsion of the Bonacolsi* (now in the Palazzo Ducale). The cathedral is a blend of different elements and styles: walls of Gothic chapels that have since been demolished, the Romanesque campanile, the right side in late Gothic style, a 16th-century interior, and a neoclassical facade.

The present *facade* was constructed between 1756 and 1761 by the Roman Nicolò Baschiera (documented from 1755 to 1770) in Carrara marble and is typically neoclassical: the central section with its four pilaster strips supports a triangular tympanum on which stand statues of saints, the work of the sculptors Giovanni Angelo Finali and Giuseppe Tivani (documented from 1752 to 1756), like the ones on top of the two lateral sections that frame the center of the facade.

The 16th-century *interior*, reconstructed after a fire that destroyed the earlier cathedral in 1545, was designed by Giulio Pippi, better known as Giulio Romano (1492/99-1546), at the request of Cardinal Ercole Gonzaga: it is subdivided into a

The facade of the Duomo, erected by Nicolò Baschiera between 1756 and 1761, and the right side which has retained its late Gothic style.

Ippolito Costa (1506-1561), Martyrdom of Saint Agatha, in the Duomo of Mantua.

Fermo Ghisoni (1507-1575), Saint Lucy, in the Duomo of Mantua.

nave and four aisles separated by Corinthian columns, with the nave covered by a coffered ceiling and decorated at the top by 16th-century statues in stucco portraying *Sybils* and *Prophets*, the work of Giovan Battista Scultori; the two inner aisles have barrel vaults and the two outer ones coffered ceilings again; a large number of chapels, closed off by railings, open onto the outer aisles.

Outstanding among these *chapels*, the work of Giovan Battista Bertani (1516-1576), who took over from Giulio Romano in 1546, and above all of Antonio Maria Viani (1555/60-1629), are, *on the right-hand side*: the first, for the presence of a 17th-century altarpiece depicting the *Miracle of Saint Giles* and, on the outside, an early Christian *sarcophagus* (4-5th centuries); the second for a 17th-century altarpiece of the *Crucifixion* and a 14th-century marble altar frontal; the third for its altarpiece portraying the *Madonna and Child with Saints*, attributed to Clemente Ruta (1685/88-1767); and the fourth, known as the *chapel of the Baptistry*, located in a Romanesque-Gothic room at the base of the campanile, which still has traces of 14th-century frescoes depicting the *Crucifixion* and, on the ceiling, busts of the Evangelists. Coming out of this last chapel, and heading toward the transept, you come to the tomb with a bas-relief portrait of the painter of Genoese origin Giovan Benedetto Castiglione, called Il Grechetto (d. in 1665). In the *transept*, a fresco portraying *The Diet of Mantua of 1459* and, on the ceiling, which has a octagonal cupola at the center, other frescoes by Ippolito Andreasi, known as Andreasino (1548-1608) and Teodoro Ghisi (1536-1601); on the altars an altarpiece depicting the *Madonna d'Itria* (end of 16th century) and the *Guardian Angel* by Domenico Mario Canuti (1620-1684).

The *apse* is decorated with the fresco *The Glory of Paradise* by Andreasino on the cupola and *The Apotheosis of the Redemption* by Domenico Fetti (1589-1623) in the vault, while the altar is flanked by 16th-century canvases depicting the *Vision of Saint John the Evangelist*, perhaps by Gerolamo Mazzola Bedoli (ca. 1500-1569) and *Christ Praying in the Garden*. Beneath the altar lies the incorrupt body of Saint Anselm, adviser to Mathilda of Canossa. His death, in 1086, is commemorated every 18 March. Other 18th-century paintings, including a *Saint Charles Borromeo* by Carlo Carloni (1686-1775), are located at the back of the choir.

From the apse you move on to the *left side of the transept*, with other frescoes by Andreasino (*The Council of Mantua in 1064*) and the *Discovery of the Most Precious Blood* by Felice Campi (1746-1817), and then to the *chapel of the Holy Sacrament*, with an octagonal plan, designed by Alfonso Moscatelli after the middle of the 17th century and frescoed by Felice Campi with *The Four Doctors of the Church* and, on the vault, a tondo depicting *The Faith*; on the walls *Saint Margaret* by Domenico Brusasorci (1516-ca. 1567) and *Saint Martin* by Paolo Farinati (ca. 1524-1606). A corridor then leads to the *Chapel of the Blessed Virgin Mary Crowned*, built in 1480, perhaps by Luca Fancelli (1430-1495), for Ludovico II Gonzaga, who wanted to transform the preexisting chapel of the

View of Piazza Broletto, with the Torre Comunale.

Blessed Virgin Mary of the Vows by dedicating it to the Madonna that used to be frescoed on the wall of a corridor linking the cathedral with the church of San Paolo, which has now been destroyed.

The side walls are frescoed with *The Death of the Virgin* and the *Descent of the Holy Ghost*, perhaps by the aforementioned Andreasino and Ghisi, while hanging in a frame on the rear wall, there is a detached fresco depicting the *Madonna and Child*. Another fresco, perhaps from 1482, of the *Madonna and Child with Saint Leonard* can be seen in the adjoining chapel.

The *sacristy*, built in 1482 and perhaps once connected with the chapel of the Blessed Virgin Mary Crowned, has a fresco of *The Mysteries of the Virgin* on the vault, by a painter of the Mantegna school (16th century) and houses two wooden sarcophagi containing the remains of Ferrante Gonzaga of Guastalla, governor of Milan and a commander of Emperor Charles V's troops, who died in 1557, and of his brother Ercole, a cardinal who distinguished himself at the Council of Trent and who died in 1563.

Other chapels are located on the *left side* of the cathedral: the first houses an altarpiece portraying *Saint Agatha* by Ippolito

Palazzo del Podestà or del Broletto, built in 1227 and also called the "Old Palace" to distinguish it from the "New" Palazzo della Ragione, built a few years later.

High relief by a 13th-century sculptor depicting Virgil Teaching, on the facade of the Palazzo del Podestà that overlooks Piazza Broletto.

The arch of the Arengario.

Costa (1506-1561), the second an altarpiece depicting *Saint Speciosa* by the above-mentioned G. Mazzola Bedoli, and the third an altarpiece portraying *Saint Lucy* by Fermo Ghisoni (1505-1575). Between the chapels stand 16th-century stucco statues from the school of Giulio Romano.

PIAZZA BROLETTO (B-2/3). Created around 1190, when the city expanded beyond its original nucleus, it is surrounded mainly by buildings from the period of the communes: the **Palazzo del Podestà**, with the **Torre Comunale**, the arch of the **Arengario**, and the **Palazzo del Massaro**.

PALAZZO DEL PODESTÀ (B-2, Piazza Broletto). Also known as **Palazzo del Broletto** and **Palazzo Vecchio**, or "Old Palace," in contrast to the "New" Palazzo della Ragione, it was built in 1227 by the Brescian Loderengo Martinengo who had been appointed podestà in Mantua. After housing the authorities of the Commune until 1272, the year in which Pinamonte Bonacolsi became lord of the city, it was damaged by fire in 1413. The building was restored by the Gonzaga in 1430 and again after 1462, perhaps with the intervention of Luca Fancelli. On the facade, as well as the inscription that records Martinengo and his deputies, Bonaccursio da Brescia and Jacopo da Bologna, there is a thirteenth-century statue of the Veronese school representing *Virgil Teaching*, wearing the

Doctor's cap and with his arms resting on a reading desk inscribed with the words "Virgilius Mantuanus poetarum clarissimus."

Piazza Erbe and the Torre dell'Orologio.

The court has late Gothic features, including a staircase that has been restored with great care. At the right-hand corner of the building rises the **Torre Comunale**. Inside it are cells for prisoners and, at the top, a belfry, which once housed the bell used to call together the citizens. At the base of the tower stands a small late-Renaissance house. A short distance away is the entrance to the **Museo Tazio Nuvolari**.

MUSEO TAZIO NUVOLARI (B-2, Piazza Broletto). Devoted to the racing car driver from Castel d'Ario (1892-1953), the museum houses documents, writings and trophies, the champion's personal effects, and contemporary photographs.

PALAZZO DEL MASSARO (B-2, Piazza Broletto). The former residence of the administrator of the property of the Commune, it now houses the bar and restaurant "Ai birri." It was once decorated with frescoes like the still visible, 15th-century one depicting Mantua surrounded by its walls.

ARENGARIO (B-2, Piazza Broletto). This large, round arch was constructed around 1300 to link the Broletto or **Palazzo della Podestà** to the **Palazzo del Massaro**, where the administrator of the commune's property resided. Surmounted by two three-mullioned windows, it has an "open-air" gallery at the top consisting of a series of small arches supported by columns. Beneath the arch, where the white stone alternates with the red of the brickwork, can be seen the iron rings that were used for the torture known as "shaking by rope," inflicted on criminals.

The interior of the Portico dei Lattonai and the late Gothic staircase in the court of the Palazzo del Podestà.

Piazza Erbe, closed at the end by the rear of the Palazzo del Podestà and on the east side by the Palazzo della Ragione with the Torre dell'Orologio.

UNIVERSITÀ DEI MERCANTI (C-2, Piazza Erbe). This 15th-century building was the seat of the university, in the sense of association, of Mantuan merchants and straddles the porticoes that provide access to Via Leon d'Oro. Traces of Renaissance paintings with figures of putti can still be seen on the facade, under the cornice.

PIAZZA ERBE (C-2). Known as "Greens Square" as it has housed the fruit and vegetable market since time immemorial, it is surrounded by buildings of different periods. It is enclosed to the north by the rear of the **Palazzo del Podestà** and to the east by the **Palazzo della Ragione** with the **Torre dell'Orologio** (Clock Tower) on the right, followed by the **Rotonda di San Lorenzo** and, at no. 26, on the far right-hand corner, the so-called **Casa del Mercante** (Merchant's House) and adjoining **Torre del Salaro**.

PALAZZO DELLA RAGIONE (C-2, Piazza Erbe). Also called "Palatium Novum" because it was built twenty-three years later than the "Old Palace," i.e. the Broletto or **Palazzo del Podestà**, which dates from 1227, it is a massive crenelated building of two stories with an external staircase that rises from the base of the Torre dell'Orologio. On the ground floor there is a 15th-century portico housing elegant stores and on the upper floor, broad three-mullioned windows that open on-

The following page:
The Torre dell'Orologio, built to the design of Luca Fancelli between 1472 and 1473.

The Rotonda di San Lorenzo, the oldest church in Mantua, built at the behest of Mathilda of Canossa in 1082.

to a single large room where justice used to be administered, now used for exhibitions; the walls still bear traces of old frescoes, depicting the siege of a castle, a *Saint Christopher and a Female Saint*, and a *Madonna Enthroned and Child with Four Saints and an Angel* signed by the painter Grixopulos (documented in 1242).

Outside the hall there used to be a sort of loggia, with access by a staircase, since demolished, which housed the **Cappella del Tribunale** (Chapel of the Law Court): a room of 5 x 6 m with a pavilion vault painted with religious scenes in the 17th century by G. B. Coccioli. The Palazzo della Ragione, restored in 1942, has a second, interesting facade at the back, overlooking Via Giustiziati.

TORRE DELL'OROLOGIO (C-2, Piazza Erbe). Built on a rectangular plan in 1472-73 to a design by Luca Fancelli, it owes its name (Clock Tower) to the old clock installed in it in 1493 by Bartolomeo Manfredi, mechanician, mathematician, and astrologer at the Gonzaga court, also known as Bartolomeo dell'Orologio.

The carefully restored dial, referred to in the old days as the *estensorio*, shows the hours, marked by Roman numerals, along with other information such as the signs of the zodiac, planetary time, the phases of the moon, and the position of the stars, so that it was possible to tell whether a certain moment of the day was under the influence of favorable planets. In the niche under the dial, made in 1639, stands a statue of *Mary Immaculate*.

The crowning part of the tower dates from 1612 and is the work of Antonio Maria Viani (1555/60-1629). From the door of the Tower there is a flight of stairs leading to the adjoining Palazzo della Ragione.

Piazza Mantegna seen from the Basilica of Sant'Andrea.

ROTONDA DI SAN LORENZO (C-2, Piazza Erbe). Set about 1.50 m below the level of the square, it is the oldest surviving church in Mantua, built in 1082 at the behest of Mathilda of Canossa. Its circular plan was probably inspired by the church of the Holy Sepulcher in Jerusalem, built by Emperor Constantine and famous throughout the Middle Ages. Closed for worship by order of Guglielmo Gonzaga in 1579 and incorporated into the adjoining buildings, it underwent restoration between 1908 and 1926. The interior, a ring-shaped nave on two stories with the women's gallery above served by two small staircases embedded in the outer wall, still has traces of 11-12th century frescoes, of Byzantine derivation, such as the *Christ the Judge* on the vault and the figures of *Angels* with richly decorated tunics visible to the left of the altar.

MERCHANT'S HOUSE (C-2, Piazza Erbe). Constructed in 1455 for the merchant Boniforte da Concorezzo from Brianza, the "Merchant's House" has a Renaissance facade with windows framed by brickwork decorations and embellished with ornamental motifs reminiscent of the Venetian style.

The brick campanile of the church of Sant'Andrea; quadrangular in shape and surmounted by an octagonal prism terminating in a conical spire, it was erected, according to two memorial tablets set in its base, between 1413 and 1414.

TORRE DEL SALARO (C-2, Piazza Erbe). Adjoining the **Merchant's House** erected by Boniforte da Concorezzo, the tower was built at the end of the 13th century and used as a storehouse for salt.

PIAZZA MANTEGNA (C-2). Adjoining Piazza Erbe and surrounded by old buildings with porticoes, it is dominated by the great arch of the **Basilica di Sant'Andrea**.

SANT'ANDREA, BASILICA OF (C-2, Piazza Mantegna). According to tradition, it stands on the site where Longinus — the soldier who struck Christ with his spear before being converted and collecting the precious blood of the Redeemer — had hidden the relic at the time of his martyrdom: the legend has it that the pots containing earth soaked with the blood of Christ were found in 804 at the point where a church dedicated to the apostle Andrew was erected, with a Benedictine monastery alongside. In 1472 Ludovico II Gonzaga obtained leave to close the monastery from Pope Sixtus IV, accusing the monks of "manifest negligence" in their custodianship of the relic, but two years earlier he had already asked Leon Battista Alberti (1404-1472) to design a "more capacious, more eternal, more worthy" temple. Owing to Alberti's death, its realization was entrusted to Luca Fancelli (1430-1495). The work continued for almost three centuries, but without straying too far from the original design.
The facade, completed by Fancelli in 1488, is rich in elements of classical architecture: the triangular tympanum, the triumphal arch, the pilaster strips with niches set between them, and the architrave. The space under the triumphal arch that leads into the basilica, serving as a vestibule, is carved with classical plant motifs, probably by local artists of the later Quattrocento.
The brickwork *campanile*, on a quadrangular plan and erected in 1413-14, is surmounted by an octagonal prism with a conical spire. The *interior*, in the form of a Latin cross, has a single nave constructed between 1490 and 1495 with a barrel vault, flanked by chapels on a square plan alternating with smaller ones roofed by cupolas. Of grandiose dimensions (103 m long, 19 m wide, and 28 m high), it is richly frescoed according to a design drawn up in the 18th century by Paolo Pozzo (1741-1803) and executed between 1785 and 1791 by local artists under the direction of Felice Campi (1746-1817) and Giorgio Anselmi (1723-1797), with scenes drawn from the Bible and the Gospels. The *dome*, constructed by Filippo Juvara (1676-1736) between 1732 and 1765, stands on a tall drum, containing twelve large windows and reaching a height of 80 m at the top of the lantern; the pictorial decoration, portraying *The Four Evangelists* and *Angels, Saints, Mantua, and Saint Longinus with the Vessels of the Most Precious Blood* is by Anselmi, while the four statues set in niches (*Faith, Hope, Charity*, and *Religion*) are by Stefano Salteri. Six chapels are ranged along the right-hand side. The first, used as the Baptistry and not frescoed, is decorated with three tondi painted in fresco detached from the entrance hall and attributed to

On the preceding page: The facade of the church of Sant'Andrea, built to the design of Leon Battista Alberti, although after 1472, owing to Alberti's death, the work was supervised by Luca Fancelli.

The interior of the church of Sant'Andrea, consisting of a single nave 103 meters in length, 19 in width, and 28 in height, covered by a barrel vault built between 1490 and 1495.

Andrea Mantegna (1431-1506)—*The Ascension*—and to Antonio Allegri called Correggio (1489-1534)—the *Holy Family* and *Deposition*. The second, dedicated to Saint Anthony, has frescoes on the wall by Benedetto Pagni da Pescia (1525-1570), an assistant of Giulio Romano, depicting *Hell*, *Purgatory*, and *Paradise*, while the altarpiece representing *Saint Anthony Reprimanding Ezzelino da Romano* is by the Mantuan painter Giulio Cesare Arrivabene (1806-ca. 1855) and dated 1846. The third chapel, frescoed in 1534 by Rinaldo Mantovano (documented from 1528 to 1539) with *Scenes of the Martyrdom of Saint Sebastian*, contains a fine 15th-century altarpiece of the Lombard school portraying the *Madonna Enthroned* and a *Saint Sebastian* by Francesco Maria Raineri known as Schivenoglia (1676-1758). The fourth chapel, frescoed by Andreasino (1548-1608) with the *Assumption* and *The Birth of the Madonna*, has a 16th-century altar frontal depicting the *Annunciation* and a wooden ancona, also from the 16th century, that frames a *statue of the Virgin Mary*. The sixth chapel is frescoed by the aforementioned Rinaldo Mantovano, to designs by Giulio Romano, with the *Crucifixion* and *The Discovery of the Most Precious Blood* and has an altarpiece depicting the *Nativity*, a school copy of an original by Giulio Romano, now in the Louvre.

The *transept* is filled with sepulchral monuments, many transferred here from other churches: in the right-hand arm the *mausoleum of the Cantelmi*, the *mausoleum of the Donati*, and the *mausoleum of the philosopher Pietro Pomponazzi*, who died in Mantua in 1525, with the *mausoleum of the prelate Giorgio Andreasi* at the end; in the left-hand arm, the *Strozzi mausoleum* (1525) and the *monument* to another prelate, *Tullo Petrozzani*, who died in 1610.

From the left-hand transept it is possible to go outside into Piazza Leon Battista Alberti to look at the side of the basilica and the remains of a medieval monastery with the arches of a 15th-century cloister.

Beneath the dome a classical balustrade prevents people from walking on the place where, in a *crypt* in the form of a Greek cross constructed in the 16th century by Antonio Maria Viani (1555/60-1629), is kept the relic of the Blood of Christ. The arch that leads into it, open only on Good Friday, when the relic is carried in procession, is decorated with a bronze bas-relief by Giovanni Bellavite (1739?-1821), located in a pavilion erected by Gian Battista Marconi (documented from 1783 to 1789). The *high altar*, constructed in 1803 to a design by Paolo Pozzo, is flanked by a 16th-century statue of Duke Guglielmo Gonzaga at prayer, while the frescoes of the presbytery depicting the *Martyrdom of Saint Andrew* are by Anselmi.

There are six chapels on the *left-hand side* of the basilica as well. The sixth (i.e. the last coming from the back of the church) houses an altarpiece depicting the *Crucifixion* by Fermo Ghisoni (1505-1575), a pupil of Giulio Romano. The fifth contains works of little significance. The fourth, known as the chapel of Mary Immaculate, has frescoes of *The Adoration of the Shepherds* and *The Adoration of the Magi* by Lorenzo Costa the Younger (1537-1583) on the walls, and, on the altar, a 17th-century wooden ancona carved by Giovan Battista Viani, brother of the better-known Antonio Maria, and two canvases by Andreasino depicting *The Announcing Archangel* and *Our Lady of the Annunciation*. In the third can be found traces of paintings from the school of Mantegna and the *sepulchral monument of the Boccamaggiore family*. The second, frescoed by Fabrizio Perla (second half of the 16th century) with the *Descent into Limbo* and the *Resurrection of Christ*, has an altarpiece of 1525 depicting the *Madonna Enthroned with Saints* painted by Lorenzo Costa the Elder (1450/60-1535). Lastly, the first chapel, dedicated to St. John the Baptist, is famous mainly because it contains the tomb of Andrea Mantegna; the walls are frescoed by his pupils, who also painted the canvases portraying *The Holy Family and the Family of John the Baptist*, *The Deposition*, and *The Baptism of Jesus*.

The dome of the church of Sant'Andrea, 80 meters tall at the summit of the lantern, was constructed between 1732 and 1765 by Filippo Juvara; the decoration of the pendentives depicts the four Evangelists.

Amidst the Splendors of the Palazzo Ducale

Extending over an area of roughly 34,000 square meters between Piazza Sordello and the lakes, the Palazzo Ducale is a complex of different buildings, constructed between the second half of the 12th century and the middle of the 17th century, when the wealth and power of the Gonzaga went into permanent decline.

For everyone who visits Mantua, this extremely complex building is an obligatory destination, in that marks of their genius have been left on it by all the artists who have worked in the city. These range from Bartolino da Novara to Antonio Pisano, better known as Pisanello, from Andrea Mantegna who produced one of his greatest masterpieces in the "camera picta" or "camera degli Sposi" to the great Giulio Romano, and from Giovan Battista Bertani to Antonio Maria Viani and Paolo Pozzo. Then there were a host of less well-known figures, such as Pompeo Pedemonte, architect of the great "hanging garden," Bernardino Facciotto, constructor between 1580 and 1581 of the "Cortile delle Otto Facce" or "degli Orsi," Bernardino Brugnoli and Giovan Angelo Barbassolo who continued the work of Pompeo Pedemonte in the "hanging garden," and Fra Zenobio Bocchi, the friar who in 1603 created the "garden of the simples," that is of herbs used in medicine, and now better known as the "garden of the pavilion."

This garden is dominated by the 15th century bulk of the Domus Nova, standing on the square dedicated to the now deceased head of the Monuments and Fine Arts Service, Paccagnini, is perhaps the main person responsible for the renaissance of the Palazzo Ducale after the decay into which it fell during the 19th century.

The oldest nucleus is represented by the buildings facing onto Piazza Sordello, the **Magna Domus** and the **Palazzo del Capitano**, which the Bonacolsi had had built. At the end of the 14th century, Bartolino da Novara erected the **Castello di San Giorgio**, and then almost a century later Luca Fancelli constructed the **Domus Nova**. Giulio Romano, who left indelible traces of his genius on Mantua, helped to enrich the Palazzo Ducale with the new buildings of the *Palazzina della Paleologa*, unfortunately destroyed at a later date, the **Appartamenti di Corte Nuova**, and **La Rustica**. Subsequently the Mantuan architect Giovan Battista Bertani, in his capacity as "master" of the duke's buildings, directed works of extension and restructuring, among other things adding the church of **Santa Barbara** to the complex. The last important interventions, spanning the 16th and 17th centuries, were those made by Antonio Maria Viani with the **Appartamento di Vincenzo I**, the **Sale delle Metamorfosi**, and the **Loggia di Eleonora**, and by Paolo Pozzo, who was responsible under Austrian rule for the work of maintenance and restoration, which had become indispensable by that time.

The Palazzo Ducale, a museum in its own right, with over five hundred rooms including the highly celebrated **Camera degli Sposi** frescoed by Andrea Mantegna, can be visited in the company of staff of the *Monuments and Fine Arts Service*, whose offices are located in the building.

On the preceding page:
Galleria dei Mesi in the
Palazzo Ducale, eastern end.

Key

Sala del Pisanello (1)

Appartamento di Guastalla (2-11)
2. Stanza delle Cariatidi/
5. Stanza delle Aquile/11.
Stanza dei Sette Scalini.

Appartamento Verde and Stanze dell'Imperatrice (12-29; A,B)
12. Camera dei Papi/13-14.
Stanze dell'Alcova/15-18.
Stanza degli Arazzi/17. Passage/
19. Camera dello Zodiaco/
20. Camera dei Falconi/
21. Stanzino dei Mori/22.
Loggetta /23. Sala dei Fiumi/
24-26. Stanze dell'Imperatrice/
A. Hanging Garden/27.
Kaffeehaus/28. Galleria dei
Fauni/29. Scala a Triangolo/
B. Cortile delle Otto Facce.

Appartamento Ducale (30-41; E)
30. Corridoio dei Mori/
31. Galleria Nuova/E. Windows
overlooking the Secret
Garden/32. Sala degli
Arcieri/33. Stanza di
Giuditta/34. Stanza del
Labirinto/35. Stanza del
Crogiolo/36. Camera di Amore
e Psiche/37. Sala degli
Specchi/38. Camera di Giove e
Giunone/39. Chapel/40. Camera
di Leda/41. Stufetta.

Appartamento del Paradiso (42-52)
42. Staircase/43-44. Stanzette
della Città/45. Gabinetto delle
Cicogne/46. Stanza dei Quattro
Elementi/47. Camerini delle
Duchesse and delle Ramate/
48. Saletta delle Piastrelle/
49. Stanza dei Paesaggi/
50. Passetto del Sole/51.
Passetto delle Frasche/
52. Scalone del Paradiso.

Giardino del Padiglione (F)

Galleria di Passerino (53-58)
53-54. Corridor/55-58. Stanze
delle Metamorfosi.

Appartamento della Mostra (59-67; G)
59. Camera di Giove/60. Stanza
delle Due Colonne/61. Camera
delle Mensole/62. Passage/63.
Sala della Mostra/64. Salone
delle Quattro Colonne/65.
Triangular passage/66. Stanza
del Pesce or di Nettuno/67.
Studio di Orfeo/G. Prato della
Mostra.

Galleria della Mostra (68)

Galleria dei Marmi or dei Mesi (69)

Appartamento di Troia (70-75; H)
70. Sala di Troia/71. Camera
delle Teste/72. Gabinetto dei
Cesari/73. Camerino dei
Falconi/74. Loggetta dei Cani/
H. Cortile dei Cani/75.
Camerino degli Uccelli/76.
Camera dei Cavalli.

Appartamento Grande di Castello (77-85)
77. Sala di Manto/78. Staircase
leading to the castle/79.
Camera dei Capitani/80.
Camera dei Marchesi/81.
Loggetta/82. Camera delle
Virtù/83. Studio/84. Stanza dei
Duchi/85. Loggia di Eleonora.

Prato di Castello (I; 86)
86. Corridore di Santa Barbara.

Castello di San Giorgio (87-103)
87. Spiral staircase/88.
Entrance hall/89. Stanza del
Fregio/90. Camera delle
Sigle/91. Sala di Esposizione
/92. Camera degli Sposi/93.
Stanza dei Soli/94. Stanza di
Mezzo
/95. Camera delle Cappe/96.
Grotta di Isabella d'Este/97.
Camera delle Armi/98.
Passage/99. Bertani's
chapel/100. Camerino
Oscuro/101. Gabinetto degli
Armadi/102. Oratory/103.
Camerino delle Stagioni.

Corte Vecchia. Ground Floor.

Scala Santa (1-2)
1. Chapel/2. Stairs.

Appartamento della Grotta (3-17; C,D)
C. Giardino Ducale/3. Arcade/
4. Arcade/5. Blind arcade/6.
Camera Grande/7. Corridor/
8. Studiolo/9. Grotta/10. Secret
Garden/11-15. Stanze di Santa
Croce/16. Church of Santa
Croce/D. Courtyard of Santa
Croce/17. Corridor and small
loggia.

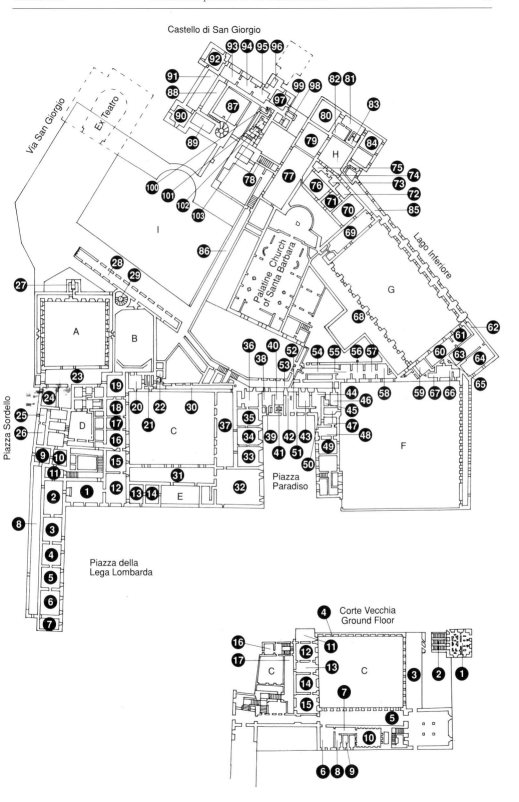

Castello di San Giorgio

Via San Giorgio

Ex Teatro

Palatine Church
of Santa Barbara

Lago Inferiore

Piazza Sordello

Piazza
Paradiso

Piazza della
Lega Lombarda

Corte Vecchia
Ground Floor

The facade of the Palazzo del Capitano.

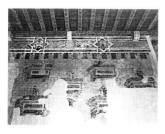

Late Gothic decoration on the walls of the Corridoio del Passerino.

MAGNA DOMUS AND PALAZZO DEL CAPITANO. Built between the last decade of the 13th century and the early years of the 14th, probably at the behest of Guido Bonacolsi known as Bottesella, Lord of Mantua from 1299 to 1309, these medieval buildings with their pointed-arch porticoes face onto Piazza Sordello: the smaller construction, without battlements, is the **Magna Domus**, while the larger, crenelated building is known as the **Palazzo del Capitano** (Palace of the Captain), after the title of the first lords of the city. The six mullioned windows on the facade of the Palazzo del Capitano were inserted around 1415, during the Gonzaga period, as a replacement for the original large windows, traces of which are still visible. A Gothic portal, under the porticoes, permits passage from Piazza Sordello to Piazza Lega Lombarda, situated behind the Palazzo del Capitano.

A visit to the over 500 rooms that make up the complex of the Palazzo Ducale commences with the 17th-century **Scalone delle Duchesse** (Grand Staircase of the Duchesses), which leads from an entrance hall located under the porticoes of the Palazzo del Capitano to the piano nobile. The first room contains the famous painting by Domenico Morone (ca. 1442-after 1517) depicting *The Expulsion of the Bonacolsi and the Triumph of the Gonzaga on 16 August 1328*. The painting shows Piazza Sordello with the facade of the cathedral that was replaced in 1756. The window offers a panoramic view of Piazza Sordello.

You then move on to the **Galleria del Passerino** (Passerino's Gallery), so called after the nickname of the last of the Bonacolsi, Rinaldo (1309-1328). This is a corridor that runs along the entire front of the Palazzo del Capitano: the Gallery was once split into a number of rooms by wooden partitions and now houses medieval marbles, memorial tablets, coats of arms, and the original of the statue of *Virgil Teaching* set on the facade of the Palazzo della Ragione (13th century), while traces of 14th-and 15th-century frescoes survive on the upper part.

A door in the corridor opens onto a staircase leading to the upper floors of the Palazzo del Capitano, where the great **Salone dell'Armeria** (Hall of the Armory, 65x15 m) is located. According to the chronicles, this was the room used for the council convened by Pope Pius II in 1459. From the Galleria del Passerino you pass into the **Appartamento della Guastalla**, whose six rooms open in succession at the back of the long corridor, overlooking Piazza Lega Lombarda; this was where the last duchess, Anna Isabella dei Gonzaga, lived from 1671 to 1703. Built in the Middle Ages and renovated in the Renaissance, with the addition of the fine wooden ceilings, they house statues from various periods: worthy of note are five terracotta statues from the school of Mantegna (late 15th century), a bust of Marchese Francesco II Gonzaga, perhaps by Gian Cristoforo Romano, and bronzes by Pier Jacopo Alari Bonacolsi known as Antico. The Gothic room contains fragments of a late 14th-century fresco depicting the *Crucifixion*

The fresco painted in the Palazzo Ducale by Pisanello around 1440, representing the knights in search of the Holy Grail at the tournament of Louverzep.

with Saints and was once used as the court chapel. The next room has a sepulchral statue of Margherita Malatesta, wife of Francesco I Gonzaga, a work from the end of the 14th century and perhaps by the brothers Jacobello and Pier Paolo Dalle Masegne (documented from 1383 to 1404).

The next room is called the **Sala del Pisanello** (Pisanello's Room), as it contains the remains of a cycle of frescoes painted around 1440 by Antonio Pisano known as Pisanello (1395-after 1450). Concealed until 1969 by later plastering and paintings, they were rediscovered by the head of the Monuments and Fine Arts Service, Paccagnini. This room is not part of the Palazzo del Capitano, but of an adjacent medieval building that used to face onto what is now Piazza Lega Lombarda. Pisanello's cycle was based on the deeds of the Knights of the Round Table in search of the Holy Grail, and in particular on the tournament of Louverzep. After looking at the *sinopie*, you proceed into the **Camera dei Papi** (Room of the Popes, mid-16th century), which once held the portraits of a number of popes, embellished with a late 16th-century fireplace in red marble from Verona. From here you move on to the **Stanze dell'Alcova** (Rooms of the Alcove) and the **Galleria Nuova** (New Gallery), a long corridor facing onto the **Cortile d'Onore** (Honor Court) of the Palazzo Ducale. Constructed at the beginning of the 17th century as an open loggia, it has now been converted into a picture gallery housing paintings from the 16-17th centuries, including: *Scenes from the Life of Saint John the Evangelist* by Gerolamo Mazzola Bedoli (ca. 1500-1569), the *Flagellation* and *Deposition in the Sepulcher* by Lorenzo Costa the Younger (1537-1583), and the *Presentation of Mary at the Temple* by Domenico Fetti (1589-1623).

From the Sala dei Papi it is possible to complete the tour of the rooms in the Magna Domus by visiting the **Appartamento degli Arazzi** (Apartment of the Tapestries), made up of three rooms and a smaller chamber which also face onto the Cortile d'Onore. This is a 16th-century wing of the building, renovated in 1780 by Paolo Pozzo (1741-1803) so that it could be used to hang the tapestries of the Flemish school depicting the *Acts of the Apostles*, acquired by Cardinal Ercole Gonzaga in 1557-59 and based on cartoons by Raphael, which had previously been kept in the Palatine Church of Santa Barbara. Each of the rooms, decorated with stuccos by Stanislao Somazzi (documented from 1768 to 1781) and pictorial ornaments by Giovan Battista Marconi (documented from 1783 to 1789), contains three tapestries and imitation tapestries by Felice Campi (1746-1817): in the first, the *Healing of the Cripple*, *The Sacrifice of Listri*, and *The Death of Ananias*; in the second, *The Fall of Saul on the Road to Damascus*, *Saint Paul Preaching in the Areopagus in Athens*, and *The Primacy of Peter)*; in the third, *The Miraculous Catch*, the *Blinding of the Sorcerer Elima*, and the *Stoning of Saint Stephen*.

Leaving the last room of the Appartamento degli Arazzi, you come to the **Camera dello Zodiaco** (Room of the Zodiac), frescoed on the vault in 1679 by Lorenzo Costa the Younger with *Diana Surrounded by the Signs of the Zodiac*; two tapestries of the French school (17th century) hang on the walls.

On the preceding page: Two rooms in the Appartamento degli Arazzi, hung with tapestries of the Flemish school based on cartoons by Raphael and formerly displayed in the Palatine Church of Santa Barbara.

View of the Hanging Garden.

The Galleria dei Fiumi, frescoed with allegorical pictures of the six rivers that flow through the territory of Mantua.

A door on the left leads into the **Sala dei Fiumi** (Room of the Rivers), which runs along one side of the so-called **Giardino Pensile** (Hanging Garden). It was built in 1575 at the behest of Duke Guglielmo Gonzaga as a hanging loggia: the pictorial decoration of six giants, realized by Giorgio Anselmi in 1775, symbolizes the rivers that flow through the territory of Mantua. The Giardino Pensile is a quadrangular space raised about 12 meters above the level of Piazza Sordello, with a portico on three sides constructed in 1579-80 by Pompeo Pedemonte and Bernardino Brugnoli, and frescoed with foliage. The portico on the left overlooks Piazza Sordello, while the one on the opposite side faces onto one of the complex's many courts. Again from the Galleria dei Fiumi, you pass into the three rooms of the **Appartamento dell'Imperatrice** (Empress's Apartment), constructed for Beatrice d'Este after the middle of the 17th century by Paolo Pozzo and used in the Napoleonic era by Eugène Beauharnais and his wife.

From the Galleria dei Fiumi and Sala dello Zodiaco, you come back to the area behind the Magna Domus, where there are several rooms decorated around 1580: the **Camera dei Falconi** (Room of the Falcons), named after the paintings on the vault, the work of Ippolito Andreasi called Andreasino (ca. 1548-1608); the **Stanzino dei Mori** (Room of the Moors), which has a wooden ceiling and a frieze decorated with Moorish figures, and 16th-and 17th-century paintings on the walls; the **Loggetta** (Balcony) and the **Corridoio dei Mori** (Corridor of the Moors, early 17th century), that runs along one side of the Cortile d'Onore, both decorated with stuccos, medallions, and grotesques. Next you come to the **Sala degli Specchi** (Room of Mirrors) that encloses the Cortile d'Onore. This was originally an open gallery built by Antonio Maria Viani (1555/60-1629) and used for receptions with dancing and music. The frescoes of mythological subjects on the vault and in the lunettes are by Francesco Borgani (1557-1624) and assistants, the mirrors are an addition of 1779, in the neoclassical style, by Giocondo Albertolli (1742-1839), while the paintings were restored by Felice Campi; of particular note are the central panels of the vault depicting *Olympus* and the *Charists of the Day and the Night*, driven by Apollo and Diana.

A door at the bottom of the Galleria degli Specchi leads into the majestic **Sala degli Arcieri** (Room of the Archers), which served as an antechamber to the private apartment of Vincenzo I and where the duke's personal guards used to be posted, armed with bows. On the walls, an altarpiece by Pieter Paul Rubens (1577-1640) portraying *The Gonzaga Family Worshipping the Trinity* (1605), unfortunately cut and damaged in the Napoleonic era when it was transferred here from the church of the Trinity; among the other paintings, the *Martyrdom of Saint Ursula* is attributed to Rubens, while the *Birth of the Virgin* is the work of Jacopo Robusti known as Tintoretto (1518-94) and his pupils and *The Multiplication of the Bread and the Fishes* is by Domenico Fetti.

DOMUS NOVA. From the Salone degli Arcieri you pass into the rooms of the **Domus Nova**, built after the middle of the

15th century by Luca Fancelli (1430-1495): according to the initial project (1480), it should have comprised four Renaissance structures arranged around an inner court, but it remained in the form of an open "U," while the court became what is now known as Piazza Paccagnini, formerly Piazza del Paradiso. The eastern wing, intended for the ducal apartments, is flanked by two towers, topped by covered roof terraces. The **Appartamento Ducale** (Ducal Apartment) was created for Vincenzo I Gonzaga at the beginning of the 17th century by Antonio Maria Viani. The first room, known as the **Stanza di Giuditta** (Judith's Room) for the four canvases depicting the *Life of Judith* by Pietro Menghi, has a gilded wooden ceiling carved with the duke's emblem, the burning crucible, used to assay the purity of precious metals. Other noteworthy paintings include the *Noblewoman at Prayer with Her Children* by Frans Pourbus (1569-1622), a *Portrait of Vincenzo II* by Justus Sustermans (1597-1681), and *Angels Playing Music* by Jacob Denys (1644-1706). The following **Stanza del Labirinto** (Room of the Labyrinth) has a labyrinthine wooden ceiling, on which the phrase "Forse che sì forse che no" ("Maybe yes maybe no") is repeated continually. This was adopted by Gabriele D'Annunzio as the title for a novel set in the Palazzo Ducale. The canvases on the wall, depicting the *Ages of the World*, are by Sante Peranda (1566-1638) and Jacopo Negretti known as Palma the Younger (1544-1628). Next comes the **Stanza del Crogiolo** (Room of the Crucible), with excellent paintings like *Saint Thomas*

The Sala degli Specchi constructed by Antonio Maria Viani at the beginning of the 17th century and frescoed with paintings of scenes from classical mythology; the mirrors, installed in 1779, are by Giocondo Albertolli.

Detail of the decoration in the Sala degli Arcieri.

amidst the Angels by Giuseppe Bazzani (1690-1769) and the *Conversion of Saint Paul* by Gerolamo Mazzola Bedoli, which leads into the **Camera di Amore e Psiche** (Room of Cupid and Psyche), so called after the subject of the painting on the ceiling, which is decorated with Baroque canvases including *Ecstasy of a Saint* by Giuseppe Bazzani. On the right, a small neoclassical room, the **Camera di Giove e Giunone** (Room of Jupiter and Juno) with another smaller room alongside, and the **Camera di Leda** (Room of Leda) adjacent to a tiny lounge (known as the *stufetta*) for winter use. This is followed by the **Scaletta di Eleonora** (Eleonora's Staircase) and the rooms of the **Appartamento di Eleonora** (Eleonora's Apartment), used by Eleonora de' Medici, who married Vincenzo I in 1584. They are not open to visitors as they now contain the offices of the Sovrintendenza: the names given to the individual rooms—**Stanzetta delle Città** (Room of the Cities), with frescoes of views of cities painted in the lunettes, **Stanza della Croce** (Room of the Cross), **Stanza dell'Angelo** (Room of the Angel), **Gabinetto delle Cicogne** (Chamber of the Storks), **Stanza dei Quattro Elementi** (Room of the Four Elements)—refer to the decoration. Finally you enter a series of small rooms known as the **Appartamento del Paradiso**

The wooden ceiling of the Stanza del Labirinto in the Domus Nova.

Detail of the decoration of the wooden ceiling of the Saletta delle Città.

(Apartment of Paradise) or **Appartamento dei Nani** (Apartment of the Dwarfs), once thought to be the accommodation for the court dwarfs, but now known to be a reproduction in miniature of the Holy Stairs in the Roman church of San Giovanni in Laterano, constructed in such a way as to oblige the visitor to walk on his or her knees. At this point you come to a new area of the Palazzo Ducale, by Giovan Battista Bertani (1516-1576) who took over the job of master of the duke's buildings from Giulio Romano (1492/99-1546).

Passing through a corridor, named after Bertani though actually dating from after the architect's death, you enter the **Appartamento delle Metamorfosi** (Apartment of the Metamorphoses). This consists of a row of four rooms along one side of the large **Giardino dei Semplici** (Simples Garden) or **Giardino del Padiglione** (Garden of the Pavilion), once reserved for the cultivation of "simples," that is medicinal herbs. The decoration of the rooms, is based on Ovid's *Metamorphoses* and dates from the 17th century.

LA RUSTICA. From here you come to another building of the Palazzo Ducale, **La Rustica**, which faces onto the **Cortile del-**

View of the Domus Nova, constructed from 1480 onward to the design of Luca Fancelli.

The Rustica and the Cortile della Cavallerizza, designed by Giulio Romano and subsequently completed by Giovan Battista Bertani.

la Cavallerizza (Court of the Riding School) and onto the lake on the other side. The architecture is by Giulio Romano and is laid out, on the side that encloses the court, on two stories: a portico in rustic work surmounted by another floor, also rusticated, with rectangular windows in spaces punctuated by spiral columns. The inner chambers make up the so-called **Appartamento dell'Estivale** (Summer Apartment), or **della Mostra** (of the Exhibition), decorated between 1561 and 1564 by Bertani and, at the end of the 16th century, by Antonio Maria Viani. The various rooms—**Camera di Giove** (Jupiter's Room), **Studio d'Orfeo**, (Orpheus' Study), **Stanza dei Pesci** (Room of the Fish) or **di Nettuno** (of Neptune), **Stanza dei Frutti** (Room of Fruits, frescoed with events and personages from the history of Mantua), **Salone delle Quattro Colonne** (Hall of the Four Columns), **Camera delle Mensole** (Room of the Consoles), **Stanza delle Due Colonne** (Room of the Two Columns)—are all richly decorated. Along the side of the Cortile della Cavallerizza runs the **Galleria della Mostra**, 65 meters long and 7 wide, constructed between 1592 and 1612 by Antonio Maria Viani to house Vincenzo I Gonzaga's art collections. The large, rectangular niches, once closed by wooden doors, held precious objects, vases, ancient sculptures, exotic curiosities, and natural history specimens.

A large awning could be used to cover the Court and was used to stage tournaments, parades, illuminations, fireworks, and even "naval battles" for the duke and his guests. The other two sides of the Court are bounded by the **Galleria dei Mesi** (Gallery of the Months) or **dei Marmi** (of the Marbles), designed, again by Giulio Romano, as an open loggia and then enlarged by Bertani and used to house ancient sculptures, and the so-called **Loggia di Eleonora** (Eleonora's Loggia), overlooking the lake.

CORTE NUOVA. The Galleria dei Mesi is already part of this area of the Palazzo Ducale, also designed by Giulio Romano, between 1536 and 1539. The group of chambers is called the **Appartamento di Troia** (Apartment of Troy), as the main room is frescoed on vault and walls with scenes from the Trojan War: the *Abduction of Helen*, the *Dream of Hecuba*, the *Judgment of Paris*, the *Arms of Achilles*, and so on. It is followed by the **Camera di Giove** (Room of Jupiter), which has the god depicted in the painting on the vault, and is also known as the **Camera delle Teste** (Room of Heads) as it used to house twelve busts of military commanders, and by the **Gabinetto dei Cesari** (Chamber of the Caesars), which once held portraits of emperors painted by Titian. These were sold by Duke Vincenzo II to the king of England, from where they went on to Spain and were destroyed in a fire at the Escorial; their place is taken today by copies made in the 16th century by Bernardino Campi (ca. 1552-1590/95). The **Camerino di Ganimede** (Chamber of Ganymede), the **Camerino degli Uccelli** (Chamber of the Birds), and the **Camerino dei Falconi** (Chamber of the Falcons) face onto the square hanging court known as the **Cortile dei Cani** (Court of the Dogs) and dedicated to the memory of "Oriana, heavenly little dog." Behind them opens the **Camera dei Cavalli** (Room of Horses), decorated on the vault with the *Fall of Icarus* and originally used to house nine canvases by Giulio Romano portraying the duke's favorite horses, now dispersed.

Detail of the decoration of the Camera delle Cappe.

The fresco depicting the "Fall of Icarus," on the ceiling of the Camera dei Cavalli.

Detail of the Camera dei Marchesi.

On the following page:
The Castello di San Giorgio, built at the end of the 14th century by Bartolino da Novara.

The Sala di Manto, with its opulent coffered ceiling and large frescoes on the walls depicting legendary episodes connected with the foundation of Mantua; among the ancient statues, the celebrated Apollo of Mantua.

Other rooms are located around the Cortile dei Cani: in order; the **Stanza dei Duchi** (Room of the Dukes), dedicated to the first Gonzaga duke, Federico II, and his successor Francesco III, and which used to house Tintoretto's canvases depicting the *Annals of the Gonzaga* (now in the Alte Pinakothek in Munich); the **Camera delle Virtù** (Chamber of Virtues); the **Gabinetto dell'Alcova** (Chamber of the Alcove); the **Camera di Apollo** (Room of Apollo); the **Loggia del Tasso** (Tasso's Loggia, where according to tradition Torquato Tasso was lodged in 1586-87); the **Camera dei Marchesi** (Room of the Marchesi), dedicated to four members of the Gonzaga family, Gianfrancesco, Ludovico II, Federico I, and Francesco II, and originally decorated with more *Annals of the Gonzaga* by Tintoretto; and lastly the **Camera dei Capitani** (Room of the Captains), devoted to the first four Gonzaga, Luigi, Guido, Ludovico I, and Francesco I, with its fresco depicting *Luigi Gonzaga Swearing the Oath of Allegiance to the People of Mantua*. From here you enter the large **Sala di Manto** (Room of Manto, late 15th century, completed by Bertani in the 16th century), with a coffered ceiling and, on the walls, eight frescoed panels depicting legendary episodes relating to the foundation of Mantua, in particular the *Legend of the Prophet Manto*; among the ancient sculptures, the so-called *Apollo of Mantua*, a Roman copy of a Greek statue from the 5th century B.C.

CASTELLO DI SAN GIORGIO, The building was erected at the end of the 14th century by Bartolino da Novara, and re-

Detail of the fresco by Andrea Mantegna depicting "The Meeting," in the Camera degli Sposi: the figures include Marchese Ludovico II and Cardinal Gonzaga.

Detail of the decoration of the Gabinetto degli Armadi.

structured in the 15th century by Luca Fancelli, who was also responsible for the **Cortile Interno** (Inner Court) with porticoes along three sides. It has a quadrangular plan with four roofed towers at the corners. It is connected with the Salone di Manto by a large staircase constructed in the second half of the 16th century by Bertani, known as the **Scalone di Enea** (Aeneas's Staircase), that leads to the Inner Court. From here you ascend to the piano nobile of the Castle by spiral ramp; this was accessible to horses as well and has spaces along its side where guards were posted. The first rooms you come to contain frescoes from various periods, taken from churches and other buildings in Mantua. Next you come to the most celebrated room in the complex, the **Camera degli Sposi** (Chamber of the Spouses), frescoed between 1465 and 1474 by Andrea Mantegna (1431-1506) for Ludovico II Gonzaga and his wife Barbara of Brandenburg: the two walls in the shade are decorated with imitation hangings of damask leather, while the other two and the vault are covered with frescoes. On the north wall, above the fireplace, Marchese Ludovico is seated alongside his wife amidst a crowd of courtiers; on the west wall, at the sides of the door, the marchese is portrayed along with Cardinal Gonzaga, other relatives, and servants with horses and dogs; in the sprandels of the vault, tondi with eight medallions portraying Roman emperors; at the center of the ceiling, a daring aerial perspective, with a circular balustrade from which *putti* and female figures peer. Adjoining is the **Stanza dei Soli** (Room of Suns), with a 15th-century fireplace attributed to Luca Fancelli and painted on the vault. It is followed by the **Stanza di Mezzo** (Middle Room), once the bedchamber of Isabella d'Este, and then the **Camera delle Cappe** (Room of Clams), so called because it is decorated with shell motifs. A small staircase leads down to the room called the **Stanzetta della Grotta** (Room of the Cave), constructed between 1490 and 1507 and embellished with a wooden ceiling carved with the emblems of Isabella d'Este. From the Camera delle Cappe you can also enter the **Cappella di Castello** (Chapel of the Castle), the work of Bertani (second half of the 16th century), and then the three **Gabinetti della Paleologa** (Paleologa's Chambers)—**degli Armadi** (of the Closets), **delle Sibille** (of the Sybils), **delle Stagioni** (of the Seasons). These are the only remaining testimonies to the house built by Giulio Romano for Margherita Paleologa, the wife of Federico II Gonzaga, and destroyed in 1899. On the upper floor of the Castello di San Giorgio there are a number of rooms used as cells, which were used by the Austrians to imprison, among others, the patriots known as the "martyrs of Belfiore." Going back up the Scalone di Enea, and leaving the Castello di San Giorgio, you can walk through the long **Corridoio del Bertani** (Bertani's Corridor) to the **Appartamento di Isabella d'Este** (Isabella d'Este's Apartment), in **Corte Vecchia** (Old Court). The marchesa had this apartment decorated when, as a widow, she decided to move out of the Castello di San Giorgio. It consists of three rooms: the **Camera Grande** (Great Chamber) or **Scalcheria** (Steward's Office), the work (1520) of Lorenzo Leombruno (1489-after 1537); the **Studiolo** (Studio), with a carved wooden ceiling; and the **Grotta** (Cave), where precious objects were kept until after 1600.

The so-called Grotta in the Appartamento di Isabella d'Este, whose walls are decorated with inlaid work in wood.

The interior on a Greek-cross plan of the Palatine Church, erected by Giovan Battista Bertani in 1562-65 as the court church for Guglielmo Gonzaga.

RIGOLETTO HOUSE. Opposite the Castello di San Giorgio, and behind the Duomo, it was given this name because it was used to stage Verdi's opera; in fact it is one of the houses for the canons of the cathedral.

PALATINE CHURCH. Part of the ducal complex, and dedicated to Saint Barbara, it was erected for Guglielmo Gonzaga in 1562-65 by Giovan Battista Bertani as the court church. You enter the basilica through a vestibule with three arches. The interior is airy: on the right-hand altar, *The Baptism of Constantine* by Lorenzo Costa the Younger, who also painted the *Martyrdom of Saint Adrian* on the left-hand altar; in the apse there is the *Martyrdom of Saint Barbara* by Domenico Brusasorci (1516-1567); on the secondary altars, *The Baptism of Christ* by Teodoro Ghisi (1536-1601) and *Mary Magdalen* by Ippolito Andreasi called Andreasino; in a chapel on the left, *Saint Louis Praying to the Virgin Mary* by Giuseppe Bazzani. The campanile, detached from the basilica, has a crown in the shape of a circular aedicule.

MUSEO DEL RISORGIMENTO. Located in Piazza Sordello, at the end of the Palazzo del Capitano, it houses objects, posters, public notices, journals, portraits, uniforms, and other documents relating to the struggle for independence.

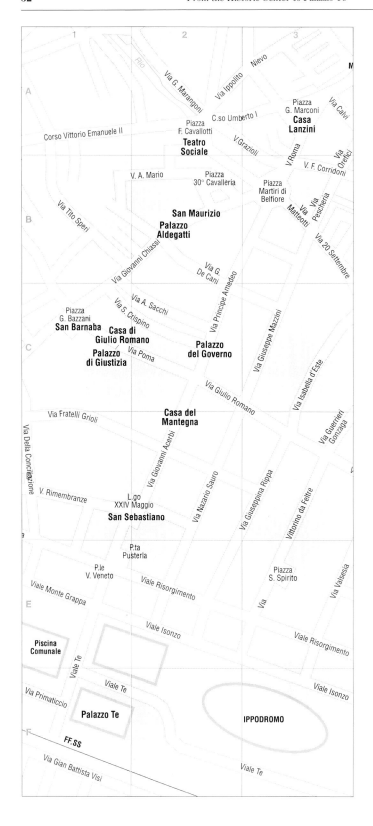

From the Historic Center to Palazzo Te

From **Piazza Sordello** you cross **Piazza Broletto** and **Piazza Erbe** to reach **Piazza Mantegna**. If you stand in front of the imposing facade of the Basilica of **Sant'Andrea**, on your left there is the **Torre del Salaro** and, in Piazza Marconi, the **Lanzini House**, the typical residence of a wealthy Renaissance merchant. Going straight along the Via Roma you come to the triangular Piazza Marconi, lined on two sides by Renaissance arcades; nearby, at the beginning of Via Goito there is a 15th century building—traces of old frescoes are still visible on its facade. The arcades continue along Corso Umberto I; with its fashionable shops, this street leads to Piazza Felice Cavallotti, where the **Teatro Sociale** is located. Opposite the theater Corso Vittorio Emanuele II begins, while on the left Corso della Libertà leads to Piazza Martiri del Belfiore; turning right here there is Via Giovanni Chiassi, which is lined with old buildings: at no. 17 there is a house with a splendid 16th century tondo consisting of a bas-relief depicting a *Virgin and Child*; at no. 10 is the house where the patriots who were executed at Belfiore used to meet—it is marked with a plaque on the facade; at no. 20 there is the 16th century **Palazzo Aldegatti** and a little further on the church of **San Maurizio**; at no. 24 there is small house with a shaped pediment which was built in 1754 and was formerly the headquarters of the pharmacists' guild; at no. 42 there is the **Palazzo dei Conti Cantoni Marca**, crowned with battlements—in its interior there is a splendid courtyard; at no. 59 there is a building with a marble portal dating from the beginning of the 16th century; at no. 61 there is the palace which formerly belonged to the **Marquises Nerli Ballati**—dating from the end of the 17th century it has a facade decorated with stuccoes.

At the point where Via Chiassi widens to form Piazza G. Bazzani there is the church of **San Barnaba**, where Via Carlo Poma begins: at no. 18 there is **Giulio Romano's House**; at no. 22 there is a 16th century building, the facade of which is adorned with a tondo depicting a *Madonna* in terracotta; opposite there is the facade of the **Palazzo di Giustizia**. At the end of Via Poma, on the left Via Principe Amadeo begins—in this street there is the **Palazzo del Governo** and, at no. 29, a late 16th century palace with a splendid marble portal—while on the right there is the beginning of Via Acerbi, in which there is the facade of the church of San Cristoforo—the church itself has been demolished—and then **Mantegna's House** and the church of **San Sebastiano**.

After passing the site of the old Porta Pusterla, which marked the limit of Mantua under the Gonzaga, and having crossed Viale della Repubblica and Viale Risorgimento—here there was formerly a canal that has now been filled in—we now come to Viale Te; the area was surrounded by the waters of the Lake of Paiolo, which was drained at the end of the 18th century and probably derives the name "Te" from the medieval term "tejetus," which was linked to the presence of "teze" (huts) or a wood of linden trees. It was in this area that the Gonzaga commissioned Giulio Romano to build a villa which was a superb example of 16th century architecture and decoration and called **Palazzo Te**.

The neoclassical facade of the Teatro Sociale, built by Luigi Canonica between 1818 and 1822.

LANZINI HOUSE (A-3, Piazza Marconi). Built ca. 1460 in Renaissance style for the merchant Ziliano Lanzini, who used it as a shop and warehouse, it boasts a facade with the windows surrounded with terracotta decorations and is surmounted by battlements.

TEATRO SOCIALE (A-2, Piazza Felice Cavallotti). Designed by Luigi Canonica (1762-1844) in neoclassical style and built between 1818 and 1822, it was originally reserved for opera, but was later also used as a cinema. The facade, with a pronaos which has six large columns and a triangular pediment, bears the inscription "Built with the Society's funds 1822." In the richly decorated interior there are three tiers of boxes and two galleries.

PALAZZO ALDEGATTI (B-2, Via Chiassi). Built in the 16th century it has a splendid marble portal and in the interior, a room embellished with a pictorial frieze attributed to Ippolito Andreasi called Andreasino (1548-1608) and other rooms with 19th century decorations.

On the following page: The Martyrdom of Saint Margaret by Ludovico Carracci, inside the church of San Maurizio.

SAN MAURIZIO, CHURCH OF (B-2, Via Chiassi). Built between 1609 and 1616, it was designed by Antonio Maria Viani, while the facade was added in 1731; it is aisleless and has an elliptical dome. In the chapels there are important paintings: in the first one on the right there is a detached 16th century fresco, *Enthroned Madonna and Saints*, and a painting by a follower of the Carracci, perhaps Lorenzo Garbieri (1580-1654), which also depicts an *Enthroned Madonna and Saints*; in the second chapel on the right there is an *Annunciation* (1615) by

The church of San Barnaba, completed in 1737 by Antonio Bibiena, who designed the facade.

Giulio Romano's house, where he lived from 1538 to 1546; a statue of Mercury stands in the niche above the front door; unusual circular windows are set in the frieze under the roof.

Ludovico Carracci (1555-1619), who also painted the *Martyrdom of Saint Margaret* and the *Torment of Saint Margaret* in the third chapel. In the apse and the choir there are paintings of the *Martyrdom of Saint Maurice* by the Flemish artist Jacob Denys (1644-1708). There are other works by Garbieri (*Saint Felicity Exhorting her Sons to be Faithful to the Virgin*, the *Slaughter of the Maccabees*, the *Martyrdom of Saint Felicity*) in the second chapel on the left, where there is also a *monument* to a cadet of the Gonzaga family (1616), while in the first chapel there is the tombstone of the *Sepulchre of Giovanni dalle Bande Nere*, the condottiere who died in battle near Mantua in 1526, and on the walls there are two paintings by Giuseppe Bazzani (1690-1769): *Pius V Exorcising a Man Possessed by Demons* and *Pius V Converting a Heretic*.

SAN BARNABA, CHURCH OF (C-1, Piazza G. Bazzani). Built between 1716 and 1736 on the site of the pre-existing church of the Order of the Servites (or Servants of Mary), designed by Doricellio Moscatelli (1660-1739) and completed in 1737 with a facade by Antonio Bibiena (1700-1774). The aisleless church was decorated with stuccoes in 1768 by the Ticino artist Stanislao Somazzi (active 1768-1781). In the interior the fourteen *Stations of the Cross* are an early work by Giuseppe Bazzani (1690-1769). Above the main door, embellished with an inner door executed in 1760 by the French artist Nicholas Thévenin, there is a painting by Lorenzo Costa il Giovane (1537-1583), the *Miracle of the Loaves and the Fishes*. In the first chapel on the right, above the baptismal font, there is a

high relief depicting the *Resurrection* (second half of the 14th century); above the third altar, also on the right, there is a wooden *Pietà* (16th century).

GIULIO ROMANO'S HOUSE (C-2, Via Poma, 18). Designed in 1540 by the artist, who supervised the building work, this house contains a room with frescoes by Giulio Romano and his pupils. The facade which Vasari described as "fantastic, all adorned with coloured stuccoes," and which originally only had two windows on each side of the door, was enlarged in 1800 by Paolo Pozzo (1741-1803), who also directed the restoration of the interior of the building. The statue of *Mercury* in a niche over the entrance door is an original from the classical era restored by Primaticcio (1504-1570). At present the house is a private residence.

PALAZZO DI GIUSTIZIA (C-2, Via Poma). Formerly the residence of a cadet branch of the Gonzaga who settled at Vescovato, near Cremona, it has a facade which was built about 1620 and is divided up by twelve giant figures supporting the capitals of the architrave; this may have been designed by Antonio Maria Viani (1555/60-1629). In the interior there is a monumental staircase (on the right of the entrance hall); various rooms were decorated by Giulio Romano's pupils, especially the courtroom with frescoes of the *Six Sages of Antiquity*, enclosed in false niches.

PALAZZO DEL GOVERNO (C-2, Via Principe Amadeo).

Palazzo di Giustizia, with facade that may have been designed by Antonio Maria Viani; the architrave is supported by twelve gigantic figures.

The exterior of Mantegna's House, with its cubic structure containing a circular court onto which face the various rooms.

Built for the Marquises Guidi di Bagno, it has an imposing facade dating from 1857 that was designed by Giovanni Cherubini (1805-?).

MANTEGNA'S HOUSE (C-2, Via Acerbi). This was begun in 1476, as is indicated by the date engraved on a marble cornerstone in the foundations, seventeen years after the arrival of Andrea Mantegna (1431-1506) in Mantua, and was probably designed by the artist himself, perhaps after he had been in contact with Leon Battista Alberti (1404-1472) and Francesco di Giorgio Martini.

The structure of the building, now that restoration work has isolated the building in an attempt to remedy the serious damage caused by previous alterations, can be seen to be very original; in fact it is in the form of a circle—the courtyard—placed in a square, or rather a cylinder in a cube. It has been suggested that the round courtyard was originally covered by a dome with a circular opening in the center, which later collapsed.

SEBASTIANO, CHURCH OF (D-1/2, Largo XXIV Maggio). Designed by Leon Battista Alberti (1404-1472) for Ludovico II Gonzaga in 1460, this church was built under the direction of Luca Fancelli (1430-1495) and has a classical plan in the form of a Greek cross. It was built on a crypt of the same shape—this was divided into small aisles by large pillars—the entrance to which consisted of five arched doorways opening onto the facade. In Alberti's plan the church was entered laterally by two flights of stairs leading to a portico, which still exists on the left-hand side of the building; the facade was divided by five large windows which corresponded to the five arched doorways. In 1925 two staircases were added to the facade, so that two of the crypt doorways were concealed and two of the windows were converted into doors. In the center of the facade there was a fresco by Andrea Mantegna (1431-1506); now there is an inscription commemorating those who died in active service.

In the interior, the *high altar* is surrounded by a marble canopy with four Tuscan columns from the 16th century; on the right there is a *sarcophagus* dedicated to the eleven martyrs of Belfiore on the left there is a *monument to the partisans* who lay down their lives in the Second World War by the sculptors Aldo Bergonzoni and Albano Seguri.

PALAZZO TE (F-1). This a large suburban villa by Giulio Pippo, better known as Giulio Romano (1492/99-1546) for Federico II Gonzaga in 1525-26. It is built on a square plan, with a central courtyard and huge garden at the rear that ends with an exedra. The visitors' entrance is on the north side, towards the city, while originally the palace was entered from the west side by a loggia, so that there was a view through the columns as far as the exedra at the far end of the garden. The facades are classical in style, with pilaster-strips, large rectangular windows and rustication obtained by placing the bricks obliquely before covering them with a thin layer of plaster. An entablature emphasizes the upper floor, with its square windows.

From the visitors' entrance, at the top of a short flight of steps, you come to an **entrance hall** and then the **Loggia delle Muse** (Loggia of the Muses) due to the presence in the

The church of San Sebastiano, commenced by Luca Fancelli to a design by Leon Battista Alberti; today it is used as a memorial chapel for the fallen.

The following page: The exterior of Palazzo Te, Giulio Romano's masterpiece, constructed as a suburban villa for Federico II in 1525-26.

The gardens surrounding Palazzo Te, separating it from the more contemporary buildings of Mantua.

One of the paintings in the Salone dei Cavalli that portray some of Federico II Gonzaga's best-loved thoroughbreds.

The large fresco in the Sala di Amore e Psiche, once used for court banquets, depicting stories of Bacchus and Ariadne as recounted by Apuleius.

lunettes of paintings representing the *Spring of Hippocrene* and the *Nymph Castalia*. Turning right from here you enter the **Sala del Sole** (Room of the Sun), the ceiling of which is divided into lozenges where there are delicate stucco figures attributed to Francesco Primaticcio (1504-1570) and Scultori; the central fresco depicts the *Sunset and the Moonrise*, while on the walls there are neoclassical stuccoes. From here you continue to the **Camera delle Imprese**, which derives its name from the *imprese* (emblems) of the Gonzaga family borne by splendid putti; on the fireplace decorated with basreliefs there is a salamander, a motif which occurs a number of times in the building.

Then follows the **Camera di Ovidio** (Ovid's Room) or **della Metamorfosi** (Room of the Metamorphoses); this is decorated with scenes from the Latin poet's work attributed to followers of Giulio Romano, such as Agostino da Mozzanega (active 1527-1539) and Anselmo de Ganis.

Turning left from the entrance hall, on the other hand, you come to the **Salone dei Cavalli** (Hall of the Horses), the largest room in the palace, which was formerly used for receptions and is decorated with frescoes depicting six enormous horses, a subject that was particularly dear to Federico II Gonzaga; above these there are scenes inspired by the *Labours of Hercules*. The ceiling is in gilded and polychrome wood, with putti, foliage, the oft-recurring salamander and the *impresa* of Mount Olympus, the dwelling place of the gods. The mountain alludes to the high peaks reached by the Gonzagas' loyalty to

The Loggia di David or Loggia Grande, separating the garden of square court of honor in the middle of Palazzo Te from the Giardino Grande; the frescoes depict scenes from the life of David.

View of the Garden with the semicircular building that closes it at the rear: in front of the coupled columns are the two pools of water of the Pescherie.

the emperor, the salamander (accompanied by the motto "quod huic deest me torquet"—"what he lacks torments me") refers to the flame of amorous passion which tormented Federico II, while the small animal was not disturbed by it.

Then proceed to the **Sala di Amore e Psiche** (Cupid and Psyche's Room), which was formerly used as a banqueting hall and is decorated with scenes from the history of Psyche, taken from Apuleius' *Golden Ass*. On the ceiling is depicted the opposition of Venus to Psyche's love for Cupid and in the lunettes the various tasks which Psyche had to perform as a punishment for having disobeyed the gods, while in the central panel of the ceiling there is the pardon and the wedding celebrated on Olympus; across two walls there is the *Wedding Feast of Cupid and Psyche* in a landscape setting; on the other walls are depicted *Venus and Mars Bathing, Mars Casting Adonis out of Venus' Bride-chamber, Bacchus and Ariadne, Polyphemus Betrayed by Aris and Galatea, Olympia and Jupiter in the Form of a Dragon* and *Pasiphaë Entering the Cow Built by Daedalus*. Besides Giulio Romano himself, these paintings were the work of his pupils Rinaldo Mantovano (active 1528-1539), Fattore, Benedetto Pagni (active 1525-1570), Luca da Faenza and Fermo da Caravaggio.

Next is the **Sala dello Zodiaco** or **dei Venti** which is much smaller; its ceiling is divided into lozenges in which there are the *Gods*, the *Months*, the *Signs of the Zodiac* and the *Winds*, while in the sixteen medallions on the upper part of the walls are depicted *Horoscopes*. Here too Giulio Romano was assisted by Rinaldo Mantovano, Benedetto Pagni, Anselmo de Ganis, Gerolamo da Pontremoli and Agostino da Mozzanega.

Then there is the small **Camera di Fetonte** (Phaeton's Room) or **Camera delle Aquile** (Room of the Eagles), which may have been Federico II's bedroom; in an octagon in the center of the ceiling there is a fresco depicting the *Fall of Phaeton* and lunettes containing *Amazons, Centaurs, Titans* and *Naiads*, while in the corners four shells form the background to *Eagles*. From this room a door leads to the so-called "duke's wardrobe," on the upper floor; ignoring this you may continue to the **Loggia di Davide** or **Loggia Grande**, which divides the courtyard from the garden with frescoes depicting the *History of David*.

The *garden*, beyond the ornamental ponds of the **Pescherie**, ends with the arches of the exedra, built in the 18th century by Paolo Pozzo (1741-1803), while on the right it is enclosed by the 17th century building of the **Fruttiere**, formerly called by the French name *Orangerie*.

At the end of the garden, on the left looking from the Loggia, is located the **Appartamento della Grotta** (Grotto Apartment). This apartment contains an octagonal vestibule decorated with grotesques, a square room decorated with history paintings (*Atilius Regulus, Horatius Cocles, Cincinnatus* and the *Judgment of Zaleucus*), a small loggia frescoed with mythological scenes, a small rectangular secret garden and, lastly, a *grotto*, in which there were formerly sculptures, mosaics and fountains.

From the Loggia di Davide it is possible to continue to the

Sala degli Stucchi (Room of the Stuccoes), with its remarkable bas-reliefs (1531) attributed to Primaticcio, arranged in two horizontal fasciae which resemble the decoration of the Roman columns from the imperial period, such Trajan's column and the Antonine column.

The next room is the **Sala dei Cesari** (Room of the Caesars) or **dell'Imperatore** (Emperor's Room), with a ceiling fresco *Caesar Ordering the Burning of Pompey's Letters* and on the walls frescoes of Roman emperors and historical episodes such as the *Continence of Scipio* and *Alexander Discovering Homer's Books*. The paintings in this room were restored in the 18th century by Felice Campi (1746-1817).

The next room, perhaps the most well-known in the Palazzo Te, is the **Sala dei Giganti** (Room of the Giants) painted by Giulio Romano and Rinaldo Mantovano with the *Victory of Jupiter over the Rebellious Titans*; the scene was intended to exalt the greatness of Charles V compared with his presumptuous enemies. The room, in which there was formerly a large fireplace, has special acoustic properties. The following rooms, known as the *Napoleonic Wing*, are decorated with stuccoes and grotesques.

The visit to the Palazzo Te also offers a good opportunity to discover the **Museo Civico** (City Museum), on the first floor of the building. Of particular interest are: the *Egyptian Collection*; the Gonzaga *Numismatic Collection*; the *Arnoldo Mondadori Gift*; the *bequest* of the painter Antonio Ruggero Giorgi (1887-1983); and the *Modern Art Gallery*.

One of the frescoes in the Sala dei Giganti, depicting the victory of Jupiter over the rebellious Titans and probably intended to celebrate the triumph of Charles V over his enemies.

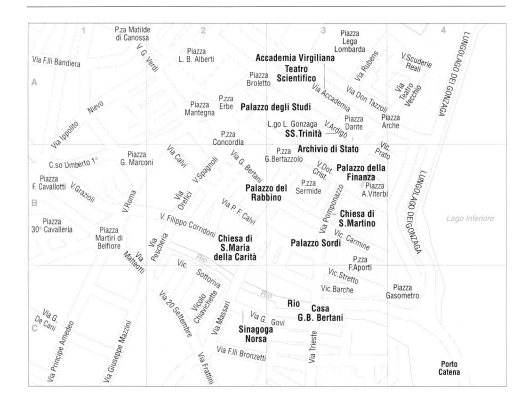

Places of Culture

Most of the buildings on these streets in Mantua date from the 17th and 18th centuries. The former, especially Palazzo del Rabbino and Palzzo Sordi, display the typological character-istics of Baroque architecture; the latter—and in particular the Biblioteca Comunale and the Teatro Scientifico, the mas-terpiece of Antonio Galli, better known as Antonio Bibiena—bear witness to the impetus given to construction in the city, after the decline of the Gonzaga, by the Austrians during the long reign of Empress Maria Teresa.

You start out from Piazza Broletto and, passing beneath the arch of the Arengario, enter Largo Luigi Gonzaga, where the former church of the **Santissima Trinità**, now closed for wor-ship, can be seen. From here you go on to Via Roberto Ardi-gò, where at no. 11, overlooked by an imposing medieval tow-er, stands the seat of the **Archivio di Stato**, with the ad-joining **Palazzo degli Studi** and, at no. 13, the entrance to the **Biblioteca Comunale**. The rooms of these three buildings contain the greater part of the documents relating to the his-tory of Mantua and to higher education in the city, so flourish-ing that between 1620 and 1779 there was a university run by the Jesuits that was authorized to confer degrees in law, the-ology, and medicine. The Biblioteca Comunale houses ex-traordinary manuscripts and incunabula, some of them illumi-nated, along with about 250,000 different works.

On Piazza Dante Alighieri, which has a statue of the poet by the sculptor Pasquale Miglioretti (1865) at its center, you find the seat of the **Accademia Virgiliana**, which incorporates the splendid **Teatro Scientifico**. On Via Accademia, after walk-ing past the Palazzo dell'Accademia in the direction of the Lago Inferiore, visible on the far side of Piazza Arche, you turn to the right to take Via Pomponazzo where, at nos. 27-31, stands the **Palazzo della Finanza**. The area in front of the Palazzo della Finanza is the one that once contained the houses of the Ghetto, the Jewish quarter: it is still possible to see, at no. 54 on Via G. Bertani, the **Palazzo del Rabbino** and, at no. 31, a building with a fine Renaissance doorway.

Returning to Via Pomponazzo, you come to **Palazzo Sordi** at no. 23 and, a little further on, the church of **San Martino**; at no. 18 there is a late 15th-century house, restructured in the neoclassical period. Turning left into Via Fondamenta, you come to the wharf of **Porto Catena**, where the Rio emerges: there is a fine view of the canal and the bridge on Via Massari. Crossing the Rio, at no. 8 on Via Trieste there is the **G. B. Bertani's House**, 16th-century architect. Coming back over the Rio again, there are two interesting 18th-century build-ings at nos. 55 and 57 on Via Corridoni. On Via Massari, after the bridge over the Rio, a fine neoclassical house at nos. 3-5. Almost opposite, at no. 11 on Via Gilberto Govi, stands the **Synagogue**. Going back into Via Corridoni, a fine 18th-centu-ry house at no. 44, the church of **Santa Maria della Carità**, and, at no. 15, the so-called **Palazzo del Ginepro** (Palace of the Juniper), a Renaissance building modified in the 18th cen-tury by Paolo Pozzo (1741-1803) and now seat of the SIP. Con-tinuing parallel to the Rio along Via Corridoni, you come final-ly to Via Roma, where the **City Hall** stands at no 39.

SANTISSIMA TRINITÀ, CHURCH OF THE (A-3, Via Ardigò). Constructed in 1597 for the powerful order of the Jesuits, it was subjected to alterations after the arrival of the French, in 1797, as well as in the last century. The occupiers transferred two famous canvases attributed to Pieter Paul Rubens (1577-1640), depicting *The Baptism of Christ* and the *Transfiguration* to Antwerp and Nancy. An altarpiece portraying *The Gonzaga Family Worshipping the Holy Trinity*, on the other hand, has been moved to the Palazzo Ducale.

ARCHIVIO DI STATO (A-3, Via Ardigò 11. *Access permitted to scholars on request*). A majestic building of medieval origin, and later modified as can be seen from the two Romanesque mullioned windows with two lights on the facade, it houses documents dealing with Mantua and its provinces from the origins to the present day. The most interesting documents are from the "Gonzaga Archives" referring to the family that held the *signoria* of Mantua from 1328 to 1707.

The exterior of the church of the Santissima Trinità, erected in 1587 for the Jesuits.

PALAZZO DEGLI STUDI (A-3, Via Ardigò). Erected by the Jesuits in 1620, as a seat for the city's university, entitled to confer degrees in law, theology, and medicine, it was reorganized in 1763 and enriched by a neoclassical facade by the architect Alfonso Torreggiani (1682-1764). After the suppression of the Jesuit order in 1773, an imperial decree prevented the university from conferring degrees in 1779. Inside the building, a grand staircase leads to the "Virgilio" junior high school and liceo and to the seat of the Biblioteca Comunale.

BIBLIOTECA COMUNALE (A-3, Via Ardigò). Set up in the Palazzo degli Studi in 1780 on the initiative of the Empress of Austria Maria Theresa, the Library, which gives pride of place to the so-called "Theresian rooms," contains over 250,000 volumes, 1200 precious incunabula, and more than 1500 manuscripts, some of them illuminated.

ACCADEMIA VIRGILIANA (A-3, Via Accademia 47. *Visit by payment: weekdays 9-12 and 15.30-18*). Established in the

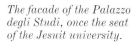

The facade of the Palazzo degli Studi, once the seat of the Jesuit university.

16th century with the backing of the pope, as the Accademia degli Invaghiti, it was later renamed Accademia dei Timidi and then degli Invitti. Maria Theresa turned it into the Reale Accademia di Scienze e Belle Arti, it was finally dedicated to Virgil on the arrival of Napoleon in 1797. The institution, which has 90 members from Italy and abroad selected from among the most eminent scholars in various disciplines and appointed by decree of the President of the Republic, is located in the **Palazzo dell'Accademia**, built to a design by Giuseppe Piermarini (1794-1808) in 1793 on the initiative of Empress Maria Theresa of Austria. The building also contains the **Teatro Scientifico**. The most famous of the rooms is the one housing the portraits of three Austrian sovereigns, Maria Theresa, Francis I, and Joseph II, painted in Vienna in 1770 by Hubert Maurer (1738-1818). An important feature is the **Biblioteca Accademica**, which contains about 80,000 volumes, with a collection of studies and rare editions of the works of Virgil; also noteworthy is the collection of 18th century surgical instruments and of drawings and prints.

The neoclassical Palazzo dell'Accademia Virgiliana, an institution whose members include eminent Italian and foreign scholars; it contains an impressive library.

TEATRO SCIENTIFICO (A-3, Via Accademia 47). Erected between 1767 and 1769 by Antonio Bibiena (1700-74) on behalf of the Accademia degli Invitti, it was then incorporated, four years later, into the building designed by Giuseppe Piermarini (1734-1808) as the seat of the Academy itself. It has an auditorium with an unusual bell-shaped plan, a fixed stage, and four tiers of boxes, all decorated with chiaroscuro paintings by Bibiena. The theater was used both for meetings of members of the Academy and for performances and concerts: the 13-year-old Mozart appeared there on 3 December 1769, and the composer's father wrote of the theater that "I have never seen anything more beautiful, of its kind, in my life."

PALAZZO DELLA FINANZA (B-3, Via Pomponazzo 27-31). Formerly a monastery of the order of the Carmelites, it was restructured in 1787 by Paolo Pozzo (1741-1803), who inserted in the facade two portals dating from the beginning of the 16th century, one from the monastery church that was later demolished, the other taken from the Customs house and perhaps the work of Giovan Battista Bertani (1516-76). Inside are two fine cloisters from the late 15th century. A few remains of the Gothic monastery church can be seen on the right-hand side of the building, on Vicolo Carmine.

PALAZZO DEL RABBINO (B-2, Via G. Bertani 54). Perhaps constructed by Frans Geffels (documented from 1635 to 1699) at the end of the 17th century, it is the most important of the surviving buildings of the old "ghetto," the quarter in which Vincenzo I Gonzaga decided to confine the city's Jews in 1612. The area, bounded by Via Giustiziati, Via Spagnoli, and Via Bertani, remained ringed by walls with four gates, open only during daylight hours, until 1798. It was then radically altered in the 19th century.

PALAZZO SORDI (B-3, Via Pomponazzo 23). Erected in 1680 by the Flemish architect Frans Geffels (documented from 1635 to 1699) for the Marchesi Sordi, who still reside in it, it has a *Madonna and Child* by Gian Battista Barberini (1625-1691) at the center of the facade and a bust of Marchese Benedetto Sordi, who commissioned the building, at the right-hand corner. Inside there is a late 17th-century monumental court, visible from the entrance way. A grand staircase leads

On the preceding page: The main facade of the Palazzo dell'Accademia Virgiliana, constructed in the neoclassical style in 1773-75 by Piermarini.

The Baroque facade of Palazzo Sordi, with alternate rusticated ashlars and a balcony over the main door; this is surmounted by a semicircular pediment containing a high relief of the "Madonna and Child" by G.B. Barberini from Como. The facade is the work of a Flemish architect active in Mantua in the second half of the 17th century, Franz Geffels.

to the piano nobile, where the two most important rooms, sumptuously decorated with stuccos and *frescoes*, , are known as the "Salone dell'età" and the "Salone di Belgrado."

SAN MARTINO, CHURCH OF (B-3, Via Pomponazzo). The reconstruction in 1737 of a preexisting medieval building, it has a high relief on the facade depicting *Saint Martin on Horseback and the Poor Man*. The altars, decorated with stucco work, have works based on the life of the saint: to the right of the choir, *Saint Martin Sharing His Cloak with a Poor Man* by Ippolito Costa (1506-1561); at the bottom of the choir, *The Mass of Saint Martin* by Giovanni Buffetti (18th century); on the left of the choir, the *Miracle of Saint Martin* by Luigi Niccolini (late 18th century). Other paintings of note are the altarpiece on the first altar on the right, a *Madonna with Saint Anthony of Padua* by Giovanni Canti (early 18th century), and the altarpiece on the third altar on the right of a *Madonna and Child with Saints*, by Lorenzo Costa the Elder (1450/60-1535).

PORTO CATENA (C-4). A basin formed by an inlet of the Lago Inferiore that was used as a river port as early as the 13th century. The name derives from the large iron chain that was used to close the harbor entrance. The waters of the **Rio**, a navigable canal constructed between 1188 and 1190, also flow into the harbor. The canal links the Lago Superiore with the

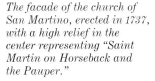

The facade of the church of San Martino, erected in 1737, with a high relief in the center representing "Saint Martin on Horseback and the Pauper."

Porto Catena, whose wharf was once used for mooring boats, on the Rio, the canal dug to connect the Lago Superiore with the Lago Inferiore.

Lago Inferiore and once marked the southern boundary of medieval Mantua.

G. B. BERTANI'S HOUSE (C-3, Via Trieste 8). Designed and constructed in the 16th century by Giovan Battista Bertani (1516-1576), it underwent substantial modifications in the last century.
On the facade there are still two original memorial tablets and Ionic columns at the sides of the entrance, one complete and the other split in half. Bertani himself had the tablets, inscribed with some comments by Vitruvius on the Ionic order, placed under the windows on the ground floor, as if to show passersby that it was the residence of an architect.

NORSA SYNAGOGUE (C-2, Via G. Govi 11). Reconstructed in 1904 on the model of the previous Synagogue, erected in the "ghetto" in 1702 and later destroyed, it incorporates sections and objects from the older building, including a wooden "Ark of the Covenant."

SANTA MARIA DELLA CARITÀ, CHURCH OF (B-2, Via Corridoni). The reconstruction in 1613 of a preexisting church from the late Middle Ages, whose aisleless plan it retains. The interior, richly decorated with stuccos in 1747, houses a series of paintings by Giuseppe Bazzani (1690-1769): three temperas on the vault, portraying the *Theological Virtues*, and eight shaped canvases on the walls depicting *Episodes from the Old and New Testament*.
Also worthy of note are an 18th-century altarpiece by Giovanni Canti on the third altar on the left, portraying a *Madonna and Child with Saints*; an altarpiece by Domenico Brusasorci (ca. 1516-1567) depicting *The Martyrdom of Saint Blaise* on the second altar on the left; and a canvas by Giovan Francesco Caroto (ca. 1480-1565) of *The Archangel Michael and Saints* in the presbytery on the left.

The exterior of the church of Santa Maria della Carità, is the 1613 reconstruction of a much older building; in the courtyard are reliefs and memorial tablets found in the territory of Mantua.

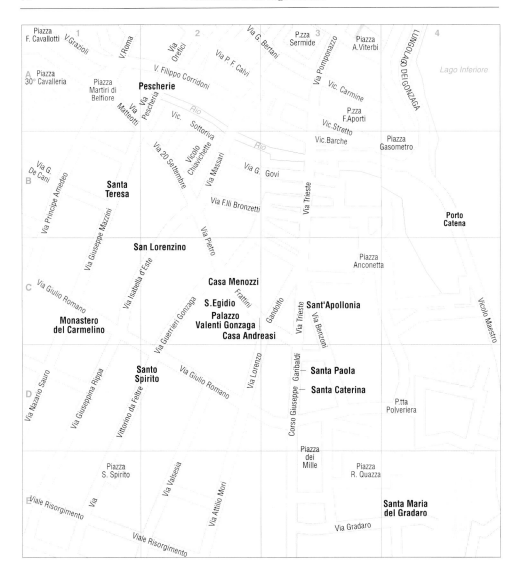

**From the Rio
to the Lago Inferiore**

From Piazza Martiri di Belfiore, on the Rio canal, you enter Via Matteotti, where you can take a look at the garden filled with sculptures (including a *Young Girl* by Aldo Bergonzoni and a *Merlin Potter* by Albano Seguri) and the isolated campanile of the church of **San Domenico**, all that remains of the sacred building, now vanished. Behind, on the other side of the Rio, the **Pescherie**, one of the works executed in Mantua by Giulio Romano; a little further on, at Vicolo Scala no. 9, a small **Gothic House** with a brickwork doorway.

From Via Matteotti you turn right into Via Mazzini; at no. 16 an interesting 16th-century **palace** with a facade remodeled in the neoclassical period; at no. 18 a neoclassical **house**; at no. 22 a **palace** that incorporates buildings from the end of the 15th century; at no. 28 a 16th-century **palace** with a Baroque staircase. Further on, the church of **Santa Teresa**.

Next turn right into Via Giulio Romano, where at no. 5 there is a fine **palazzo** renovated in the 18th century by Paolo Pozzo, and just after it the former **monastery of the Carmelino**, now the seat of the Istituto Magistrale (Teacher's Training School). Turn to the left into Via Isabella d'Este, where at no. 13 stands the church of **San Lorenzino**, now an Evangelical church. Turning to the right again, you enter Via Pietro Frattini, which contains the following interesting buildings: at no. 1 an 18th-century **palace**; at no. 5 **Menozzi House**; at no. 7 **Palazzo Valenti**; and at no. 9 **Andreasi House**. Almost opposite, the church of **Sant'Egidio**, from where you can take Via Guerrieri Gonzaga and then Via Vittorino da Feltre, which widens to form a square in which the church of **Santo Spirito** stands. From here, returning to Via Giulio Romano and then turning right, you come to Corso Garibaldi and Piazza dei Mille, where there is a monument to the national hero, the work of Pietro Bordini (1887). Over a wall you can see the facade of the church of **Santa Paola**, closed for worship, while the beautiful medieval church of **Santa Apollonia** (restored after 1781 and completed with a neoclassical facade in 1834) is located on nearby Via G. Benzoni. A little way past Piazza dei Mille, you find the church of **Santa Caterina** and, on Via Gradaro, the church of **Santa Maria del Gradaro**. This church is one of the oldest in Mantua and one of the best loved by its inhabitants, who greeted with joy the completion of the works of restoration, in 1966. This permitted worship to be resumed in the building, which had fallen into serious decay after, following application of the laws on the supression of the monasteries in 1772, it had been used by the Austrian military authorities as an ammunition depot. Turning to the right and then to the left into Via S. Allende, you arrive at Vicolo Maestro, which runs along the shore of the Lago Inferiore. The panorama is very suggestive. Turning to the left, along the edge of the lake, you come to Porto Catena.

PESCHERIE (A-2, Via Pescheria). Buildings erected in 1535 to designs by Giulio Romano (1492/93-1546) as a place for the sale of fish connected to the meat market—the "Beccherie"—and then demolished in the 19th century. All that remains is a double rusticated portico, with round arches, that spans the Rio and is surmounted by an attic, also rusticated.

SANTA TERESA, CHURCH OF (B-1, Via Mazzini). Constructed in 1668 alongside the monastery of the same name, it has a facade subdivided by pilaster strips and a beautifully decorated, barrel-vault portal. Inside, six large canvases by Filippo Gherardi (late 17th century) depicting *Scenes from the Life and Martyrdom of Saint Theresa*. Part of the adjoining monastery was used, during the years of Austrian rule, as a chapel in which prisoners condemned to death used to receive the last sacraments: the martyrs of Belfiore, among others, passed through it before their execution.

CARMELINO, MONASTERY OF THE (C-1, corner of Via Giulio Romano and Via Nazario Sauro). It is used today by the Istituto Magistrale named after Isabella d'Este—to whom the sculptors Albano Seguri and Selvino Sabbadini have devoted works situated in the adjoining garden. It has a fine cloister from the late 15th century. The deconsecrated church now houses the Archivio Storico Comunale.

Above: The exterior of the 15th-century Menozzi House; below, the exterior of the 15th-century Andreasi House. Both were designed by Luca Fancelli.

SAN LORENZINO, CHURCH OF (C-2, Via Isabella d'Este). Erected in 1590, probably by Giuseppe Dattaro known as Pizzafuoco (1540-1619) and used as a private chapel by the Petrozzani family, it has an unusual elliptical plan. It is currently used by the Evangelical Church.

MENOZZI HOUSE (C-2, Via Frattini 5). Built in the second half of the 17th century to a design by Luca Fancelli, it has a three-story facade; the terracotta statues set in the five niches on the upper story are copies of works from the Mantegna school that are now in the Palazzo Ducale.

PALAZZO VALENTI GONZAGA (C-3, Via Frattini 7). Commenced in the second half of the 17th century and never completed, it has an impressive facade, attributed to Nicolò Sebregondi (ca. 1580/90-1652), with five rows of windows. It is characterized by the contrast between the rusticated marble ashlars of the socle and the brickwork of the upper section. In the courtyard, on which Frans Geffels probably worked, the windows are underlined by a sumptuous, stucco-work decoration. Inside only the rooms of the first floor have been finished, decorated with frescoes and stuccos by G. B. Barberini from Como.

ANDREASI HOUSE (C-3, Via Frattini 9). The home of the Blessed Osanna Andreasi (1449-1505), it was designed by Luca Fancelli in the second half of the 15th century. On a basement of unplastered brick that was restored in 1926, rises the facade with three rows of windows and the entrance sur-

On the preceding page: The Rio with the Renaissance building of the Pescherie, constructed by Giulio Romano and once used to house the fish market.

The exterior of the church of San Lorenzino, erected in 1590 as a chapel for the noble Petrozzani family; the interior is on an elliptical plan.

The 18th-century facade of the church of Sant'Egidio, erected on the site of a preexisting building.

mounted by a round-headed arch. On the two upper floors are the rooms where the Blessed Osanna used to go into retreat, preserved in their original state. A corridor on the ground floor leads to a small inner court, split into two parts by a transverse portico with three arches supported by columns that have the family coat of arms on their capitals.

SANT'EGIDIO, CHURCH OF (C-3, Via Frattini). An 18th-century reconstruction of an older building, it has a facade with half columns. Inside, on the second altar on the right, a *Deposition of Christ with Cardinal Ercole Gonzaga* by Ippolito Costa (1506-1561) and, on the third altar on the left, the *Vision of the Blessed Osanna Andreasi*; at the bottom on the right, in the Magnaguti chapel, formerly that of the Marchesi Valenti, a *Madonna and Child with Saints* by Benedetto Pagni (1525-1570), a follower of Giulio Romano; behind the high altar, a *Martyrdom of San Vincenzo* (1776), by Giuseppe Bottani (1717-1784). On the paving there is an inscription where Bernardo Tasso, the father of Torquato, was buried.

SANT'APOLLONIA, CHURCH OF (C-3, Via G. Benzoni). Erected in the Middle Ages as Santa Maria in Betlemme, then reconstructed after 1781 and completed by a neoclassical facade in 1834, it contains a number of valuable paintings: on the first altar on the right, a *Madonna and Child with Two Saints* (first half of the 16th century); on the first altar on the left an 18th-century altarpiece of the Venetian school depicting *San Bernardino and the Apostles Peter and Paul*; at the bottom of the apse, an 18th-century altarpiece by Giuseppe Bottani (1717-1784) portraying the *Holy Family and Saints*; on the right of the presbytery, a *Madonna and Child* by Francesco Borgani (1557-1624).

SANTO SPIRITO, CHURCH OF (C-3, Via Vittorino da Feltre). Recently subjected to major modifications, it contains the remains of pictorial decorations from the late 15th century and a wooden monumental altar. In the small square in front, a memorial tablet records Vittorino da Feltre, a humanist who lived at the Gonzaga court from 1423 to 1445.

SANTA PAOLA, CHURCH OF (C-3, Corso Garibaldi). Constructed in late Gothic style in the first half of the 15th century as the church of the monastery of the same name, at the behest of Paola Malatesta, wife of Gianfrancesco Gonzaga.

SANTA CATERINA, CHURCH OF (D-3, Corso Garibaldi). The reconstruction in 1738 of a preexisting medieval church, it has a facade that blends curved lines and neoclassical elements. The old campanile, isolated from the rest of the building, is clearly visible from a courtyard at Vicolo Santa Caterina 1.

SANTA MARIA DEL GRADARO, CHURCH OF (E-3, Via Gradaro). Built in the middle of the 13th century on the site, according to tradition, of the martyrdom of Longinus, a Roman soldier who brought from Palestine to Mantua a handful of earth soaked in the blood of Christ, it was originally a church of the Canons Regular of Saint Mark and then, from 1454 onward, of the Benedictines of Monte Oliveto. Substantially renovated during the Renaissance, at the time of the suppression of the monasteries, after 1772, it was used as a storehouse by the Austrian military government. The work of restoration made it possible for the church to be reopened for worship in 1966. The sloping Romanesque facade, broader than it is tall, has a large central rose window and small hanging arches beneath the cornice, while the two openings in the form of pointed arches present a foretaste of the Gothic style. The portal, dating from 1295, is the work of the Veronese architects "Jacobus" and "Gratasola Ognabenus." The interior, with a nave and two aisles, is Gothic in style with its ogive arches, supported in the front part of the church by cylindrical columns of brickwork, and in the rear part, reserved for the monks and closed off by a wall of which a few traces remain, by quadrangular pillars. The remains of the pictorial decoration of 1513-14 are still visible in the aisles. The presbytery contains important frescoes in the Byzantine style from the middle of the 13th century, depicting the *Last Supper* and *Jesus, Saints, and Prophets*; in a bay on the left of the presbytery there is a 14th-century fresco portraying *Jesus and Saints*. Adjoining the church is the cloister, also restored, closed on one side by a Renaissance building constructed after 1454.

The facade of the church of Santa Caterina, on which curvilinear elements are mixed with neoclassical ones, reconstructed in 1738.

The lean-to facade, with its elegant rose window and pink-and white striped portal, of the church of Santa Maria del Gradaro.

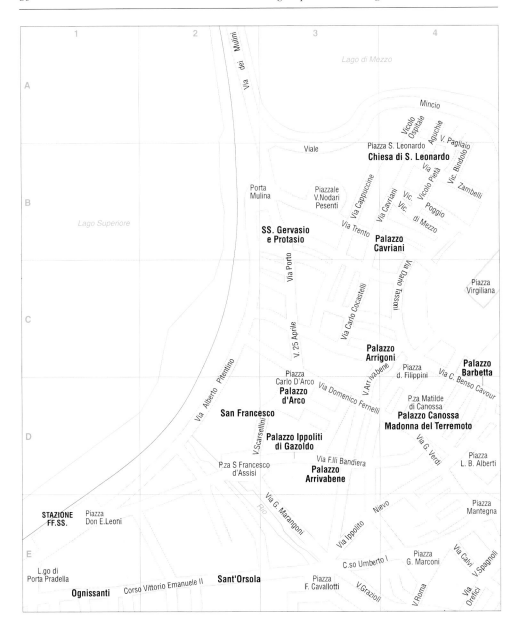

From the Rio
to the Lago Superiore
and the Lago di Mezzo

From Piazza F. Cavallotti, straddling the Rio, you walk along Corso Vittorio Emanuele II in the direction of the Lago Superiore. On the corner with Via Corrado there is a pillar carved at the end of the 15th century, at no. 12 a fine building dating from 1912, and at no. 52 a 16th-century **palace** with a beautiful garden open to the public and a graceful neoclassical facade. On the corner of Via Ivanoe Bonomi, the church of **Sant'Orsola**, and then, at no. 122, a building whose facade bears a marble fascia dating from 1481 alongside cornices and balconies from the 19th century. Further on, almost at the end of the Corso, the church of **Ognissanti**, from where you may carry on toward the **Valletta dei Belfiore**. Going past the junction with Via della Conciliazione, you come to Viale Tazio Nuvolari and the Lago Superiore. From Viale Nuvolari, and Piazza Don E. Leoni, named after a martyr to the Nazis, where the railroad station is located, you pass into Via Solferino and Via San Martino, where at no. 21 there is a fine 17th-century **palazzo**, and arrive at the church of **San Francesco**. Taking Via Scarsellini, you come to Piazza Carlo d'Arco, dominated by the imposing **Palazzo d'Arco**, undoubtedly worth a thorough visit to the interior as well, and in particular to the Salone dello Zodiaco frescoed by Giovan Maria Falconetto.

In the nearby Piazza San Giovanni, there is a 19th-century **palazzo** at no. 7 and a late 15th-century **house**, unfortunately heavily tampered with, at no. 3.

Going back toward the Rio, you enter Via Fratelli Bandiera, where at no. 23 you can see **Palazzo Ippoliti di Gazoldo**, at nos. 18-20 **Palazzo Arrivabene**, at no. 17 a **building** from the 13th to 15th centuries, and at no. 27 a **house** built in 1611, with neoclassical additions. A short distance away stands the Renaissance **Palazzo Arrigoni**.

At the end of the street, in Piazza Matilde di Canossa, you can admire **Palazzo Canossa**, the 18th-century church of the **Madonna del Terremoto**, and a **palace**, also dating from the 18th century, with a portico. On nearby Via Cavour, at no. 13, stands another noble **palace** built for the counts of Canossa and known as the **Albergo Reale** or **Palazzo Barbatta**.

To complete the itinerary, you can proceed along Via Trento, where at no. 16 there is the impressive **Palazzo Cavriani** (see below) and further on, almost at the end of the street, the church of **Santi Gervasio e Protasio**. From here you can go on to **Porta Giulia**, the work of Giulio Romano.

Returning to Palazzo Cavriani, it is worth walking along the side of the building down Via Alessandro Cavriani, where you can see a 15th-century **palace** with a porticoed court at no. 4, and a fine crenelated **palace** at no. 8, until you reach the open space in front of the church of **San Leonardo**.

The church of Sant'Orsola, built in 1608 to a design by Antonio Maria Viani as part of a monastery that was later demolished.

The church of Ognissanti, the result of alterations made to a preexisting building in 1752; it contains fine paintings and fragments of 14th-century frescoes.

SANT'ORSOLA, CHURCH OF (E-2, Corso Vittorio Emanuele II). Constructed in 1608 to a design by Antonio Maria Viani (1555/60-1629), as a church for the adjacent monastery (demolished in 1930). It has a late Renaissance window, with projecting half columns and a triangular pediment that contrasts with the interior on an octagonal plan. There is a remarkable 17th-century painting above the high altar, attributed to Lanfranco.

OGNISSANTI, CHURCH OF (E-1, Corso Vittorio Emanuele). The reconstruction in 1752 of a preexisting medieval building, of which survive the original **campanile** and the **Cappella dei Morti** (Chapel of the Dead)́, (it contains ancient tombs). The church has some valuable works, including an 18th-century altarpiece by Giovanni Cadioli (1710-1767) depicting the *Miracle of Saint Mark* on the first altar on the right, a 16th-century altarpiece from the school of Giulio Romano depicting *The Sermon of John the Baptist* on the first altar on the left, a *Madonna and Saints* by Nicolò da Verona (documented from 1462 to 1493), and a *Saint Benedict and Saint Clare* by Ippolito Andreasi called Andreasino (1548-1608) in the apse.

VALLETTA DI BELFIORE About 1 km from the church of **Ognissanti** and from Porta Pradella, which used to mark the western boundary of the city. It has gone down in history as the place where the Austrians executed ten Italian patriots. It is now hemmed in by new constructions and marked by a simple monument with the inscription "Falling here the martyrs of freedom overthrew their executioner."

SAN FRANCESCO, CHURCH OF (D-2, Via Scarsellini). Built between the end of the 13th century and 1304, on the site where an oratory already stood that had been constructed for Frate Benvenuto, one of Francis's disciples, it was consecrated in the presence of Pope Pius II in 1459. Chosen as a burial place by several members of the Gonzaga family and other Mantuan nobles, it was closed for worship by the French in 1797 and turned into a storehouse, deteriorating to such an extent that many of the sepulchral monuments were transferred to Sant'Andrea and other churches. After further damage by Allied bombing in April 1945, the church was reconstructed in 1951-52 in its original form, apart from some uncertainty over the apse. The spire that used to stand at the top of the campanile was replaced by battlements during the 19th century. The interior, with a nave and two aisles separated by brickwork pillars and a ceiling of trusses in the Gothic manner, contains a large number of chapels: the first on the right, from the 15th century still has the remains of frescoes by Stefano da Verona (1374/75-after 1438) and Domenico Morone (ca. 1442-after 1517) depicting *Scenes from the Life of Saint Francis*; the third chapel has a wooden altar from the late 16th century and traces of a fresco portraying *Saint Francis and Saint Bonaventure*; the fifth chapel holds an 18th-century wooden altar as well as a painting of *Saint Francis* attributed to Pier Francesco Maz-

The church of San Francesco, constructed between the end of the 13th century and the beginning of the 14th on the site where once stood an oratory dedicated to one of Francis of Assissi's disciples, Frate Benvenuto.

zucchelli known as Morazzone (1573-1626) and another work of the Venetian school, *Saint Francis at Prayer*. The most famous chapel is the one known as the "cappella dei Signori" or "dei Gonzaga," which once housed numerous sepulchral monuments and still has fragments of the 14th-century decoration depicting *Scenes from the Life of Jesus*. On the back wall is a *Saint Louis of Toulouse* attributed to Tommaso da Modena (1326-1379), in which Luigi Gonzaga, founder of the dynasty and Lord of Mantua from 1328 to 1360, appears among the entourage of figures. Alongside the door of the campanile, there are the remains of a 14th-century fresco of *Christ Crucified*. In the left-hand aisle fragments of other cycles of frescoes with *Scenes from the Nativity*, allegories on the *Church and the Heresies*, a *Madonna with Worshipping Figures*, and the *Damned*.

PALAZZO D'ARCO (D-3, Piazza Carlo d'Arco, *open from 9 to 12; on Saturday and Sunday from 15 to 17 as well*). Erected in 1784 by Antonio Colonna for Conte Gherardo d'Arco, a nobleman originally from Trent, it came into the possession of the Fondazione d'Arco in 1973, after the death of the last heir of the Mantuan branch of the family, Giovanna Guidi di Bagno, and was turned into a museum. The palace is made up of three blocks arranged around a semicircular court, closed by an exedra, and also comprises two Renaissance buildings acquired by the d'Arco family in 1872. These are currently being restructured and

View of the exterior of Palazzo d'Arco, built in 1784 by Antonio Colonna for the family of the Conti d'Arco.

Detail of the semicircular inner court of Palazzo d'Arco.

one will be used to house Conte Luigi d'Arco's **collection of scientific instruments**. Work is also being carried out on the **Biblioteca** (Library), which contains over 6,000 volumes, including manuscripts, and 3,000 prints. Climbing the imposing grand staircase, embellished with antique chests bearing the family coat of arms and a sedan chair, you come to the **Salone degli Antenati** (Hall of the Ancestors), housing the 60 family portraits from the 16th century onward; in the showcases, ceramics and precious objects collected by the Conti d'Arco. A door on the right leads into the **Sala delle Prospettive Architettoniche** (Room of Architectural Perspectives), decorated with archeological landscapes in the neoclassical style and furnished with 18th-and 19th-century furniture. This is followed by the **Camera dei Ritratti** (Chamber of Portraits), with paintings of noblewomen and noblemen from the 15th to the 19th centuries, the **Camera delle Nature Morte** (Chamber of Still Lives), with genre paintings of the 17th and 18th centuries, the **Sala della Musica** (Music Room), containing precious instruments, and the **Loggetta** with a small collection of sculptures, including the basin of a fountain from the destroyed villa of Marmirolo.

From the Salone degli Antenati you can enter the rooms of the **Pinacoteca** (Picture Gallery): the **Sala di Diana** (Room of Diana); the **Sala Rossa** (Red Room), furnished in the Victorian style and containing a photograph of Contessa Giovanna; the **Sala di Pallade** (Room of Pallas Athena); the **Sala Verde** (Green Room) or **Sala della Giustizia** (Room of Justice), which has a *Madonna and Child with Angels* attributed to Nicolò da Verona (documented from 1462 to 1493); the **Passetto dei Religiosi** (Passage of the Religious), decorated with two paintings by Alessandro Magnasco (1667-1749) portraying *Hermits at Prayer*; the **Sala delle Figurazioni Sacre** (Room of Sacred Representations), with paintings of religious subjects including a *Madonna* attributed to Bernardino Luini (1480/90-ca. 1532), a *Christ with the Cross* perhaps by Sodoma, and a *Christ Crucified* by Anthony van Dyck (1599-1641); and the **Sala di Ales-**

sandro **Magno** (Room of Alexander the Great), with seven 18th-century canvases by Giuseppe Bazzani (1690-1769) based on the life and deeds of the Macedonian conqueror, and a *Flight into Egypt*. From the **Sala Verde**, through a small neoclassical room and an internal staircase, you descend to the court. In one of the two Renaissance buildings, you can see the **Cappella dei Conti d'Arco**, with an 18th-century altar, and on the upper floor, the **Salone dello Zodiaco** (9.70 x 15.4 m), frescoed in 1520 by Giovan Maria Falconetto (1458-1534) with the symbols of the constellations against a backdrop of famous works of architecture, such as the Colosseum and Arch of Janus in Rome, the Arena in Verona, and the Mausoleum of Theodoricus in Ravenna.

PALAZZO IPPOLITI DI GAZOLDO (D-3, Via Fratelli Bandiera 32). Erected in the first half of the 18th century, it has a grand staircase and beautiful rooms furnished with period furniture.

PALAZZO ARRIVABENE (D-3, Via Fratelli Bandiera 18/20). Attributed to Luca Fancelli (1430-95) and constructed from 1481 onward, as we are informed by an inscription on the base of the corner tower. It has a fine inner court with a Renaissance portico and open gallery. The upper part of the building at no. 20 was added in the 18th century.

PALAZZO ARRIGONI (C-3, Via Arrivabene 18). Constructed during the Renaissance and acquired by the Marchesi Arrigoni in the 17th century, it is a two-story building attributed to Luca Fancelli (1430-1495). Passing through the main entrance, you come to a portico with five arches supported by marble columns that faces onto an inner court. The external windows on the second floor are coupled in the Renaissance manner.

The corner tower and facade of the 15th-century Palazzo Arrivabene, attributed to Luca Fancelli.

The facade of Palazzo Canossa, with its facing of imitation rustic work; at the base of the columns flanking the main door and supporting a balcony, stand two marble dogs, emblems of the Canossa.

The exterior of Palazzo Cavriani, erected in the 18th century by the Bolognese architect Alfonso Torreggiani.

The church of Santo Gervasio e Protasio, with its 19th-century facade designed by Giovan Battista Vergani.

Santa Maria del Terremoto, erected in 1759 on the site where, during an earthquake in 1693, the Virgin Mary appeared to the faithful.

PALAZZO CANOSSA (D-4, Piazza Matilde di Canossa). Built on the ruins of a preexisting building that belonged to the Alberigi in the second half of the 17th century for the noble Canossa family, originally from Verona, whose residence it was until the middle of the last century. It now houses a school. The articulation of the building on two floors and the decorative motifs take their inspiration from Giulio Romano. At the sides of the main entrance, two columns with marble dogs, the symbol of the family, at their bases support a balcony.

MADONNA DEL TERREMOTO, CHURCH OF THE (D-4, Piazza Canossa). The name of the church (Madonna of the Earthquake) refers to the place where the Virgin Mary appeared after the earthquake of 1693, on which it was erected in 1759. On the side walls inside hang two canvases by Giuseppe Bazzani (1690-1769): a *Nativity* and a *Pietà*.

PALAZZO BARBETTA (C-4, Via Cavour 13). Built for the Canossa in 1784, it was used for some time as a hotel—whence the name of "Albergo Reale" (Royal Hotel) by which it is sometimes known.
It was designed in the neoclassical style by Giovan Battista Marconi and has an interesting rusticated facade built out of unplastered brick.

Porta Giulia, once a lookout and defensive position, designed in the Renaissance style by Giulio Romano.

Below: The facade of the church of San Leonardo, built in the 12th century and subjected to alterations in 1793.

PALAZZO CAVRIANI (B-4, Via Trento 16). Constructed around 1756 by Alfonso Torreggiani (1682-1764), it has a majestic grand staircase and rooms decorated with frescoes and with antique furniture and works of art. Opposite the building, there is a neoclassical garden, laid out after 1826 by Giovan Battista Vergani (1778/1788-after 1841), with a statue of Virgil at its center that Marchese Luigi Cavriani commissioned from the Milanese sculptor Stefano Girola, who also carved the busts of illustrious Mantuans set on the pillars of the railings.

SANTI GERVASIO E PROTASIO, CHURCH OF (B-3, Via Porto). Reconstructed out of preexisting buildings by Giovan Battista Vergani (1778 after 1841), who completed the new facade in 1836, it retains the original Romanesque campanile from the 12th century. Inside, there is an altarpiece portraying *Three Saints* by Giovanni Canti on the first altar on the left, and in the presbytery and the *Vision of Saint Martin* attributed to Domenico Fetti (1589-1623).

PORTA GIULIA. Erected in 1549 to the design of Giulio Romano (1492/99-1546), it served as a lookout post and defense. The arch has a barrel vault and is topped by an elegant triangular pediment. A little way off, on the left, stands the monument to Andreas Hofer, a hero of the Tyrolese resistance against Napoleon, shot here by the French in 1810.

SAN LEONARDO, CHURCH OF (B-4, Piazza San Leonardo). The reconstruction in 1793 of a preexisting Romanesque building, of which the 12th-century campanile survives, it incorporates the 15th-century chapel of San Gottardo. Inside there is a fresco by Lorenzo Costa the Elder (1450/60-1525) depicting *The Redeemer and Prophets* and, on the high altar, a *Madonna and Saints* (early 16th century) attributed to Francesco Raibolini called Francia (1460-1517) an important.

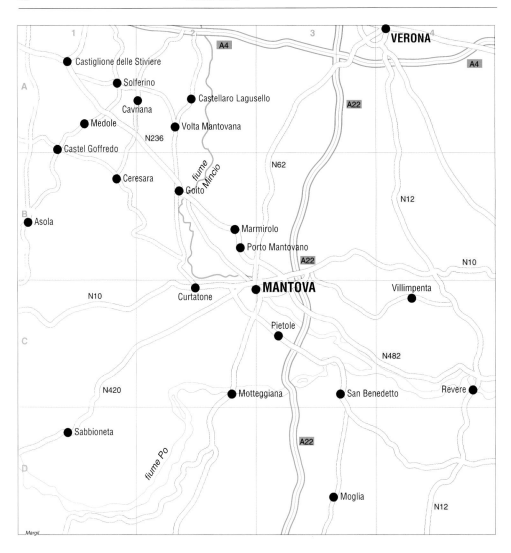

The Environs

The enlightened influence of the Gonzaga and of their splendid court, frequented by so many men of culture and artistic geniuses, has also left its mark on all the surroundings of Mantua, both in churches and sanctuaries like **Santa Maria degli Angeli** and **Santa Maria delle Grazie**, and in numerous villas like the **Favorita**, at Porto Mantovano, and the hunting lodge of **Bosco Fontana**, at Marmirolo. In the 15th century Luca Fancelli, Alberti's successor in Mantua, was very active in the province as well.

At **Motteggiana**, 18 km from Mantua, there is a villa, now privately owned, embellished with a hanging court served by an imposing flight of steps.

At **Revere**, 35 km from the city, there is the splendid **Palazzo Gonzaghesco**, erected for Ludovico II in 1460 and now used as the offices of the local authority.

At **Ceresara**, 28 km from Mantua, the **Palazzo di San Martino Gusnago**, at present in private hands, was the result of a commission from Luca Fancelli by Francesco Secco, the son-in-law of Ludovico II; the interior is decorated with paintings from the school of Mantegna. A few years later it was Giulio Romano who was making his mark on the surrounding region as well, working on, among other things, the parish church of **San Benedetto Po**, 20 km from Mantua, the **mausoleum of Baldassare Castiglione** located in the first chapel of the **Sanctuary of Santa Maria delle Grazie** at Curtatone, 7 km from Mantua on the road to Cremona, the villa of the **Galvagnina Vecchia** near Moglia, 35 km from Mantua, the **Villa Longhi-Visentini** at Villimpenta, 22 km away, and **Corte Spinosa** at Porto Mantovano, only 4 km from the city.

Other places of outstanding importance are **Pietole**, traditionally regarded as the birthplace of Virgil, and the **Parco delle Bertone**. A trip to **Sabbioneta**, situated in the angle formed between the left bank of the Po and the lower course of the Oglio, is almost indispensable. Its spendor is due to Vespasiano Gonzaga's decision, in the middle of the 16th century, to turn it into a sort of "ideal town," although it then gradually fell into decay, almost as if, as one writer has put it, "the flow of history appears to have come to stop" within its walls. There are many beauties to admire at Sabbioneta: the Palazzo Ducale with its rooms filled with artistic treasures, the Palazzo del Giardino or Casino del Giacinto the prince's private villa, the unusual Galleria degli Antichi or "Corridor Grande," used to house Vespasiano's precious art collections, and the Teatro Olimpico, erected by Vincenzo Scamozzi in 1588 on the lines of the similar masterpiece in Vicenza designed by his great master Andrea Palladio. For once, the religious buildings are almost overshadowed, even though of considerable quality. They include the parish church of Santa Maria Assunta, the church of the Incoronata, the church of San Rocco, and the church of the Beata Vergine del Carmine.

With time at your disposal, it is also worth making a visit to a number of other localities in the Mantua region: Asola, Castel Goffredo, Castellaro Lagusello, Castiglione delle Stiviere, Cavriana, Goito, Medole, San Benedetto Po, Solferino, and Volta Mantovana.

The sanctuary of Santa Maria delle Grazie in the locality of Curtatone, on the outskirts of Mantua and along the highway to Cremona.

SANTA MARIA DEGLI ANGELI, CHURCH OF. Situated in the suburb of degli Angeli, on the road for Cremona, it is a construction in the Gothic style dating from 1429. Inside, there is a panel depicting the *Madonna degli Angeli* on the high altar, perhaps the work of Nicolò da Verona.

SANTA MARIA DELLE GRAZIE, SANCTUARY OF. Situated about 7 km from Mantua along the Cremona road, in the locality of **Curtatone**, Francesco I Gonzaga had it erected between 1399 and 1406. The church is an example of Lombard Gothic, with the facade characterized by a portico with thirteen round-headed arches and lunettes frescoed in the 16th century. The portico houses memorial tablets from various periods and some cannon balls collected during the battle of Pavia (1522) between King Francis I of France and Emperor Charles V. Inside, a series of wooden loggias and niches runs along the side walls, which were used to house wooden, stucco, and wax statues and other objects donated to the sanctuary "for grace received." From the ceiling, with a cross-vault frescoed in the 15th century with floral motifs, hangs a stuffed crocodile in chains, perhaps a symbol of the disease subdued and rendered harmless.

The nine chapels are of great interest. On the right-hand side, the first is the family **Chapel of the Castiglioni** with the mausoleum of Baldassare Castiglione; designed by Giulio Romano, it has epigraphs by Pietro Bembo and Baldassare himself; on the vault, *frescoes* from the school of Giulio Romano, and on the right, the mausoleum of Camillo Castiglione, who died in 1598. In the second chapel, there is an altarpiece depicting the *Martyrdom of Saint Lawrence*, by Lorenzo Costa the

Younger (1537-1583). In the third chapel a wooden *ancona* with painted panels (early 17th century), probably the work of the brothers Antonio Maria (1555/60-1629) and Giovan Battista Viani. In the apse, frescoed with the *Coronation of the Virgin Mary and Prophets*, there are two paintings by Giuseppe Bazzani (1690-1769) of the same subject, the *Madonna in Heaven*. Going back toward the exit, the first chapel on the left-hand side contains a 16th-century altarpiece representing *Saint Jerome* and a sepulchral monument dating from 1498. In the next chapel, an altarpiece by Francesco Bonsignori (1455-1519) portraying *Saint Sebastian* and a sepulchral monument from 1525. Another sepulchral monument from the early 17th century leads to a chapel of the same date, while the last chapel contains a large altarpiece depicting the *Martyrdom of Saint Hippolytus*, by Lattanzio Gambara (ca. 1530-1573/74), and the *mausoleum of the Marchesi Ippoliti di Gazoldo* (1595).

FAVORITA Situated in Porto Mantovano, this is a 17th-century villa, now in ruins, constructed between 1613 and 1624 by Nicolò Sebregondi (1580/90-ca. 1652) for Francesco Gonzaga, who intended to transfer the ducal court there. The death of Ferdinando in 1626, the "sack" of Mantua by the landsknechts four years later, and the abandonment of the building, followed by its partial demolition during the 19th century and further damage from a fire in 1913, have reduced the villa to its present state of decay. All that is left is the central block with two fine loggias.

BOSCO FONTANA. Located about 5 km from Mantua, at **Marmirolo** on the highway to Brescia, it consists of about 200 hectares of woodland. The name (Fountain Wood) derives from the presence of a spring. Today it is a nature reserve. In a clearing in the middle of the wood stands the **hunting lodge** of the Gonzaga, constructed in the same architectural style as Palazzo Te: a quadrangular building, with cylindrical towers at the corners and, at the center of each of the two facades, a loggia with three large arches surmounted by a triangular pediment. Built between the end of the 16th century and the beginning of the 17th by Giuseppe Dattaro (1540-1619) and Antonio Maria Viani (1555/60-1629) for Duke Vincenzo I, it is still surrounded by a moat filled with water.

PIETOLE. A village outside the old Porta Cerese, about 5 km from the end of Corso Garibaldi, it has been identified with the "Andes" where Virgil was born in 70 B.C. A monument inaugurated in 1884 in the presence of Giosué Carducci celebrates the poet. There is also a small **museum** in the locality, housing archeological finds from the zone.

PARCO DELLE BERTONE. Situated 14 km from Mantua, on the highway for Brescia, the park covers almost 7 hectares. Footpaths wind amongst centuries-old trees. A villa built in 1870 now houses the offices of the authority in charge of the Parco Naturale del Mincio.

On the following page: The Gonzaga Villa della Favorita, constructed by Nicolò Sebregondi at Porto Mantovano between 1613 and 1624 for Ferdinando Gonzaga.

The 26 arches of the Galleria degli Antichi, in the Sabbioneta, which Vespasian had used to house his collection of statues.

SABBIONETA. An "ideal town" created from 1564 onward by Vespasiano Gonzaga (1511-1591), who personally directed the work in collaboration with a series of "masters." Visits to the town, with its characteristic hexagonal plan and projecting star-shaped bastions, are guided by staff of the local tourist board and commence from one of the two openings in the walls, Porta Vittoria (1560) and Porta Imperiale (1579), which provide access to the road system made up of streets at right angles to one another. The most important building is the **Palazzo Ducale** also known as "Palazzo Grande," constructed between 1568 and 1577; the facade has five arches over classical rustic work and the interior is decorated with frescoes. Worthy of mention among its numerous rooms are the **Gabinetto di Diana** (Diana's Room), the **Sala dei Dardi** (the Dardis Room), the **Salone delle Aquile** (Hall of Eagles), housing four equestrian statues of Vespasiano and his forefathers in suits of armor; the **Sala d'Oro** (Golden Room), with a fine fireplace and a ceiling decorated with pure gold leaf; and the **Galleria degli Antenati** (Gallery of the Ancestors) containing twenty-one sculptures by Alberto Cavalli, including *Phaethon*, *Mars*, and *Mercury*.

On the same square stands the church of **Santa Maria Assunta** (1580-92). This has a single nave and frescoes by Giorgio Anselmi (1723-1797), paintings by Bernardino Campi (ca. 1522-1590/95), and works by Antonio Galli called Bibiena (1700-1774). Another important church is that of the **Incoronata** (1586-1588), on an octagonal plan with a cupola, which houses the mausoleum of Vespasiano Gonzaga by Giovan Battista della Porta, with a bronze *statue* of the duke, the work of Leone Leoni (1509-1590).

Outstanding among the secular buildings is the **Teatro Olimpico** (1588-90), by Vincenzo Scamozzi (ca. 1552-1616). The interior is rectangular in plan, with walls decorated with frescoes of the Veneto school, like the two large *Vedute* of Rome at the sides of the parquet.

The **Galleria degli Antichi** (Gallery of the Ancients) or **Corridor Grande** (Grand Passage) is most unusual: a portico about one hundred meters long, made up of 26 arches, in which Vespasiano Gonzaga had set out his collection of sculptures, under cover. The duke's private residence, the **Palazzo del Giardino** also known as the "Casino," is worth a visit. Constructed between 1577 and 1588, its rooms are frescoed with mythological subjects by Bernardino Campi and his pupils.

CASTEL GOFFREDO. The seat of a cadet branch of the Gonzaga, the town grew up around the **castle**, already in existence, from 1480 onward. It has a fine square with porticoes onto which face **Palazzo Gonzaga Acerbi** (15th century, remodeled in the 18th), flanked by two towers.

CASTELLARO LAGUSELLO. A town of fairly ancient origin (finds from the Bronze Age have been made there), surrounded by walls overlooking a lake, it still contains many of the stone houses that were built around the **Gonzaga-Tacoli castle** (13th century, modified after 1391).

The church of the Immacolata in Sabbioneta.

CASTIGLIONE DELLE STIVIERE. An important Etruscan center, and then Roman *castrum*, it became a domain of the Visconti and, from 1404 onward, of a cadet branch of the Gonzaga. It is the birthplace of St. Louis Gonzaga (1568-1591). Noteworthy: the **Palazzo della Pretura** (Magistrate's Court, 15th century); the **Basilica of San Luigi**, which Francesco Gonzaga had built in honor of his brother in 1612 and which houses the silver urn containing the saint's skull as well as a number of works of art, including a canvas portraying *Saint Louis at Prayer* by Antonio Balestra (1666-1740); the **house of the saint's birth**; the **Collegio delle Nobili Vergini di Gesù**, founded in 1608 and the seat of the **Museo Storico Aloisiano**; the 18th-century **Palazzo Triulzi-Longhi**, since 1959 the seat of the **Museo della Croce Rossa Internazionale**.

The church of San Luigi in Castiglione delle Stiviere.

GOITO. Ancient fortified village, with the "checkerboard" layout of streets, in which are located: **Villa Giraffa**, a restructured Capuchin monastery; the Baroque church of **San Pietro**; the Neo-Gothic **Villa d'Arco** (18th century) surrounded by a large park that overlooks the Mincio.

SAN BENEDETTO PO. An agricultural center that developed around the **Abbey of Polirone**, founded in 1007 by the Benedictines. The abbey, which had been taken over by the Cistercians in the meantime, was enlarged by the Gonzaga, who invited Giulio Romano to work on the church dedicated to Saint Benedict between 1537 and 1546. The facade is a portico with a loggia in which are set statues of *Adam*, *Eve*, and *David* by Antonio Begarelli (1499-1565). It was altered in the 18th century with the addition of a neoclassical loggia. The *interior*, made up of naves, with a ceiling decorated with simulated coffers in the Mannerist style, is flanked by ten chapels frescoed by artists of the school of Giulio Romano and ornamented by statues by Begarelli and his studio. The *choir* is noteworthy, with stalls carved in 1550 by Vincenzo Rovetta (1515-?). The *sacristy* contains the *tomb of Mathilda of Canossa*, although her body was moved to Rome in the 17th century; the walls are frescoed by pupils of Giulio Romano. The abbey complex includes the Romanesque church of **Santa Maria**, with a fine *mosaic pavement* dating from 1511; the **chiostro dei secolari** (cloister of the seculars, 15th century); the **refectory** (1478) with a *fresco* (1513-14) attributed to Antonio Allegri known as Correggio (1489-1534) and a *Last Supper* by Girolamo Bonsignori (died in 1529); the **chiostro dell'infermeria** (cloister of the infirmary), frescoed in the 16th century with *Scenes from the Life of Saint Simeon*; the **library** (1790); and the **Museo Civico Poliriano**.

The Polyronian abbey at San Benedetto Po, with the church built by Giulio Romano and enlarged between 1537 and 1546.

VOLTA MANTOVANA. Grown up around a medieval **castle**, the town still has its **walls**, pierced by a Gothic *arch*. The **parish church** contains 17th-century canvases depicting the *Nativity of the Virgin*, and there are two villas belonging to the Gonzaga, **Villa Cavriani** (16th century) and **Villa Venier**.

Bibliography
R. Berzaghi, *Il palazzo Ducale di Mantova*, Milan 1992.
P. Carpeggiani, *Mantova, profilo di una città*, (with Sabbioneta and San Benedetto Po), Mantua 1976.
P. Carpeggiani, "Mantova," in AA.VV., *Itinerari per la lombardia*, Rome 1982.
P. Carpeggiani, I. Pagliari, *Mantova. Materiali per la storia urbana dalle origini all'Ottocento*, Mantua 1983.
R. Castagna, *Mantova nella storia e nell'arte*, Mantua 1979.
E. Marani, *Sabbioneta e Vespasiano Gonzaga*, Sabbioneta 1977.
G. Paccagnini, *Il Palazzo Ducale di Mantova*, Turin 1969.
G. Paccagnini, *Il Pisanello e il ciclo pittorico cavalleresco di Mantova*, Milan 1971.
M. R. Palvarini, C. Perogalli, *Castelli dei Gonzaga*, Milan 1983.
C. Perogalli, *Castelli della Lombardia*, Milan 1969.
C. Tellini Perina, *Sabbioneta*, Milan 1991.

Printed for Electa
by Fantonigrafica-Elemond Editori Associati